The Sonnets

A BLAISDELL BOOK
IN THE HUMANITIES

EDITED BY
George Lyman Kittredge

Revised by Irving Ribner

William Shakespeare

The Sonnets

BLAISDELL PUBLISHING COMPANY

A Division of Ginn and Company

WALTHAM, MASSACHUSETTS · TORONTO · LONDON

PREFACE

The New Kittredge Shakespeares

The publication of George Lyman Kittredge's *Complete Works of Shakespeare* in 1936 was a landmark in Shakespeare scholarship. The teacher who for almost half a century had dominated and shaped the direction of Shakespearean study in America produced what was recognized widely as the finest edition of Shakespeare up to his time. In the preface to this edition Kittredge indicated his editorial principles; these allowed a paramount authority to the Folio of 1623 and countenanced few departures from it while, at the same time, refusing to "canonize the heedless type-setters of the Elizabethan printing house." Kittredge's work was marked by a judicious conservatism and a common sense rarely found in equal measure in earlier editors of Shakespeare. In the thirty-odd years which have gone by since the appearance of this monumental volume, however, considerable advances have been made in the establishment of Shakespeare's text, and our body of knowledge about the dates, sources, and general historical background of Shakespeare's plays has vastly increased. The present revision is designed to apply this new knowledge to Kittredge's work so that it may have as much value to the student and general reader of today as it had to those of thirty years ago.

Before his death Kittredge had issued, in addition to *The Complete Works,* separate editions of sixteen of the plays, each copiously annotated. Some of the notes were unusually elaborate, but they interpreted Shakespeare's language with a fullness and precision attained by few other commentators, for Kittredge had few equals in his intimate knowledge of Elizabethan English. In freshly annotating the plays I have, accordingly, tried to use

Kittredge's own notes as fully as space would permit. Where I have repeated his distinctive language or recorded his characteristic critical opinions, I have followed the note with the symbol [κ]; where Kittredge's definition of a term can be found in essentially the same words in other editions, I have not used the identifying symbol. Every annotator draws upon the full body of the notes of earlier editors, and to give credit for every note is impossible. Notes have been placed at page bottoms.

The brief introductions which Kittredge wrote for the plays have been replaced by new ones, for what seemed like indisputable fact some thirty years ago often appears today to be much more uncertain, and many new issues of which Kittredge was not aware have been raised in recent criticism. The new introductions seek to present what are now generally agreed to be basic facts about the plays and to give some indications of the directions which modern criticism has taken, although specific analyses of individual plays are avoided.

Such great authority attaches to Kittredge's text that it has not frequently — and never lightly — been departed from. Where changes have been made, they have usually involved the restoration of copy-text readings now generally accepted in place of the emendations of eighteenth- and nineteenth-century editors of which Kittredge, in spite of his extraordinary conservatism in this regard, sometimes too easily approved. Only rarely has an emendation been adopted in the present revision which was not also adopted by Kittredge. All departures from the copy-texts are indicated in the notes, emendations followed by the names of the editors by whom they were first proposed. Wherever Kittredge's text has been departed from for any reason, his reading is given in the notes. Modern spelling has in a few instances been substituted for Elizabethan forms which are mere spelling variations but which Kittredge nevertheless retained. His punctuation has not been altered except in a few very rare instances.

The system of recording elisions and contractions which Kittredge explained in his introduction to *The Complete Works* has been retained, as has his method of preserving to the fullest the copy-text stage directions, with all additions to them enclosed within square brackets. Although modern editors recognize the vagueness of the place settings of Elizabethan plays and are reluctant to include the place designations so favoured by eighteenth- and nineteenth-century editors, much historical interest nevertheless attaches to these, and Kittredge's place designations accordingly have been retained between square brackets. Kittredge's attempt to retain the line numbering of the Globe text, which resulted in considerable irregularity in prose passages, has been abandoned, and the lines of each play have been freshly numbered. Kittredge's act and scene divisions have been retained, as has his practice of surrounding by square brackets those divisions which are not in the copy-texts.

The plan of *The New Kittredge Shakespeares* is a comprehensive one. They will include a new edition of *The Complete Works* and individual editions of each of the plays, the sonnets, and the poems. A comprehensive introduction to Shakespeare's life, times, and theatrical milieu will be published both as a separate volume and as an introduction to *The Complete Works*.

IRVING RIBNER

INTRODUCTION

The Sonnets

◇◇◇◇◇
◇◇◇◇◇
◇◇◇◇◇ That Shakespeare's sonnets are among the greatest love poems the world has ever seen is obvious to all, but there are few other statements one may make with equal certainty about them. So numerous are the problems they present and so intriguing the mysteries inherent in them, with their teasing implications about the life of a genius about whose personal affairs we know so little, that they have been the subject of endless speculation and have given rise to countless volumes of commentary. Most of this material is assembled and digested in the massive two-volume Variorum edition by Hyder E. Rollins (Philadelphia: J. B. Lippincott, 1944), to which every editor of these poems must be indebted. The many problems have been more recently surveyed in editions by Edward Hubler (New York: McGraw-Hill, 1959), O. J. Campbell (New York: Schocken Books, 1964), W. G. Ingram and Theodore Redpath (London: University of London Press, 1964), and John Dover Wilson (Cambridge: Cambridge University Press, 1966). The present edition will attempt only to present the basic facts and to suggest some of the more important theories which scholars have constructed upon them.

PUBLICATION

Our earliest reference to Shakespeare as a writer of sonnets occurs in 1598. Francis Meres in that year published his *Palladis Tamia: Wits Treasury,* in which he referred to Shakespeare as the author of comedies and tragedies comparable to those of the classical poets, and as an example of his carrying on the "wittie soul of Ovid," offered the evidence of "his *Venus and Adonis,*

his *Lucrece,* his sugred Sonnets among his private friends." In
the following year two of the sonnets (numbers 138 and 144)
were printed, almost certainly without Shakespeare's authorization and probably without his knowledge, by William Jaggard
in a small octavo volume called *The Passionate Pilgrim by
William Shakespeare.* The twenty poems in this volume are
headed by Shakespeare's two sonnets and include also three poems
taken from the fourth act of *Love's Labours Lost* and fifteen
poems which are not by Shakespeare at all. That some sonnets
by Shakespeare were in private circulation by 1598 we can thus
be sure, but just how many there were and at what date he had
begun to write them are problems which continue to perplex the
scholars. Of the 154 sonnets in our collection we can merely say
with Kittredge that "the dates of the rest are not to be determined. They must have been written at different times and on
miscellaneous occasions throughout Shakespeare's literary life
from ca. 1592 to 1609." Some scholars would date them as early
as 1588.

On May 20, 1609, Thomas Thorpe entered in the Stationers'
Register "vnder thandes of master wilson and master Lowndes
Warden a Booke called Shakespeare sonnettes" and in the same
year published a quarto edition (Q) of 154 sonnets. Of the eleven
copies of this quarto which have survived, four state on their
title pages that they are to be sold by William Aspley and seven
that they are to be sold by John Wright, indicating merely that
Thorpe had contracted with two separate booksellers for the dis-
tribution of his volume. The printing was done by George Eld.

We may be fairly certain that Thorpe's volume, with its
puzzling dedication to "Mr. W.H.," was not published with
Shakespeare's authorization or approval. Where Thorpe derived
his copy we do not know, and there is little point in adding here
to the innumerable conjectures which scholarship has produced.
The identity of Mr. W.H. is also a matter about which we can
only conjecture. While some scholars have suggested that the
initials may be those of whatever person supplied Thorpe with
his copy, others maintain that they are the initials of the "fair
youth" to whom the bulk of the sonnets were written. Although

the matter is of crucial importance, it is unlikely that it will ever be entirely resolved.

There is reason to believe that Thorpe's edition of the sonnets was suppressed by higher authority and withdrawn from circulation, not a surprising development if Mr. W.H. was indeed a powerful nobleman not likely to be pleased by the publication of private poems written to him by a friend of humble social station. The sonnets were not printed again until 1640, in which year all but eight of them were included by John Benson in a volume called *Poems: written by Wil. Shakespeare Gent.* Benson rearranged the sonnets in groupings under various headings, thus inaugurating a tradition of rearrangement which various editors have pursued up to our own day.

THE ORDER OF THE SONNETS

When Edmund Malone prepared the first great modern edition of the sonnets in 1780, he followed Thorpe's quarto of 1609, and this order and numbering of the sonnets has been adhered to in most later editions, including the present one. Although Thorpe seems to have been a careful editor who tried to follow his manuscript copy, it is likely that his arrangement does not entirely reflect the sequence in which the sonnets actually were written, and it may obscure the continuity of theme from sonnet to sonnet which was generally a feature of sonnet sequences. Attempts to restore Shakespeare's order have accordingly been a major preoccupation of scholars.

In general the poems may be divided into two large groups. Sonnets 1 through 126 are written, for the most part, to a young man who is the poet's friend; sonnets 127 through 154 are written either to or about a woman who is dark in complexion, has been the mistress of the poet, and has betrayed him by entering into some kind of liaison with the poet's friend. Of the first large group, sonnets 1–17 form a close and homogeneous unit in which the poet in each poem urges his friend to marry and have children. In sonnets 18–126 the poet continues to celebrate his affection for his friend, while various sonnets introduce other themes,

sometimes closely related and sometimes not. The poet's preoccupation with a "rival poet" who is apparently seeking the
young man's patronage also appears in this group of sonnets,
particularly numbers 79–86.

In the second major group of sonnets (127–54) editors have
generally found far less unity of theme, although there are clearly
certain sonnets which have close connections with certain others.
It has been virtually impossible to argue that Thorpe's arrangement of these sonnets could possibly represent Shakespeare's in-
tention. The most persuasive attempt at rearrangement has been
that of Brents Stirling in *Shakespeare 1564–1964,* ed. by Edward
A. Bloom (Providence, R.I.: Brown University Press, 1964). By
assuming that Thorpe worked with a manuscript consisting of
fourteen leaves, with two sonnets on each leaf, and that in the
course of composition certain of the leaves were misplaced,
Stirling has arranged these twenty-eight sonnets so that they fall
into three closely related groupings. First there is a series of six
sonnets, arranged in pairs, on the theme of "My Mistress' Eyes":
140–139, 153–154, and 130–127. Then follow eight sonnets dealing
with the poet, his friend and his mistress, which should be read
in the following order: 144, 143, 135, 136, 131, 132, 133, and 134.
Finally there are eleven sonnets on the theme of "Perjury of Eye
and Heart" which should be read in the following order: 137,
141, 142, 149, 150, 151, 152, 147, 148, 129, 146. Sonnets 128, 138,
and 145 are independent. Stirling's theory is intriguing, in part
because it rests largely upon bibliographical evidence rather than
upon the predilections of individual editors, which govern so
many of the other rearrangements that have been proposed.

THE VOGUE OF SONNETEERING

Shakespeare's sonnets represent the greatest and perhaps the last
expression in England of a vogue for sonnet writing which
reached its climax in the last decade of the sixteenth century.
Although the origins of the sonnet form are somewhat obscure,
having probably originated among the poets of twelfth- or
thirteenth-century Provence, the writing of sonnet sequences was
established in Italy by Francesco Petrarca (1304–1374), who

wrote two series of sonnets, comprising 317 poems in all, in which he expressed his love for an idealized woman named Laura, celebrating her both alive and after her death. Whether or not Petrarch actually loved such a person is not certain and is ultimately unimportant, for what he expressed was the exaltation of a neo-Platonic ideal of beauty, and his sonnets came to embody conventional attitudes of the lover to his lady — her cruelty, his suffering, his inability to sleep because of her, and so on — as they were embodied in the chivalric love code of his own time.

Petrarch was imitated in France by such poets as Ronsard, Desportes, and DuBellay, who echoed his specific themes and attitudes, making "Petrarchism" itself the object of their efforts. Early in the sixteenth century the Petrarchan sonnet was introduced into England by Sir Thomas Wyatt upon his return from Italy. Henry Howard, Earl of Surrey, developed the specific English form of the sonnet which was to be used by Shakespeare, replacing the multiple-rhymed Petrarchan octave and sestet with three alternate rhyming quatrains and an epigrammatic couplet, a form much more appropriate to the specific character of the English language. The sonnets of Wyatt and Surrey were published in *Tottel's Miscellany* of 1557.

The vogue of the sonnet sequence was given great impetus by Thomas Watson, who in 1582 published a sequence of 100 sonnets as *Hecatompathia,* or *A Passionate Century of Love.* The artificiality which had come to mark the sonnet form may be seen in the very pride which Watson takes in the conventional, imitative quality of his work. Of even greater influence was *Astrophel and Stella,* published in 1591, the sonnet sequence addressed by Sir Philip Sidney to Penelope Devereux, in which, while Sidney reflected on his own relations to the woman who should have been his wife, he expressed also the conventional Petrarchan attitudes which by his time had become virtually inseparable from the sonnet form.

By 1595 virtually every poet in England had written or was writing sonnets. Edmund Spenser addressed his *Amoretti* to Elizabeth Boyle, who was to be his wife, but most poets expressed their Petrarchan commonplaces in supposed adoration of entirely imaginary ladies or of noble patronesses whom they flat-

tered under various pseudonyms. Thus Daniel addressed his
sonnets to Delia, Drayton to Idea, and Constable to Diana. By
the turn of the seventeenth century so many sonnet sequences
had been written, and so many variations had been rung upon
the Petrarchan commonplaces, that the form may be said to have
suffocated in its own excesses. Although it never died out, and
poets like Donne were soon to revitalize it and give it new directions, the great vogue of sonneteering had had its day by 1600.

What is truly remarkable about Shakespeare's sonnets is that,
although they appear to have been written while the vogue was
at its height and were published soon after it had subsided, they
are utterly unlike any of the sonnets of his contemporaries. They
are addressed mainly to a young man rather than to an idealized lady; they are not exercises in sterile Petrarchan commonplaces but instead express powerful emotion in terms which have
an unmistakable ring of sincerity; they appear to express an intimate relation among four people: the poet himself, the young
man to whom he writes, the poet's mistress, and a rival poet.

It is thus no wonder that few commentators have been able
to resist the temptation to explore the biographical implications
of Shakespeare's sonnets. That they would throw considerable
light upon the personal life of the poet if we could understand
them fully is obvious. Yet in our speculations we must observe
the word of caution of those critics who have argued that Shakespeare, the greatest dramatist the world has ever known, was
entirely capable of forging a love story in his sonnets with no
necessary relation to events in his own experience. Of such critics,
Kittredge has been among the more notable:

> In treating the Sonnets as material for Shakespeare's biography,
> we should not forget that we are dealing with the supreme dram-
> atist — with that extraordinary genius who, beyond all others, could
> put himself in the place of any human being, man or woman, and
> then could make that person express thoughts and feelings and
> passions as he or she would have uttered them if endowed with
> superhuman power of expression. In a sonnet, both from its very
> nature and from the conventions that attend it, the author must
> seem to "unlock his heart." He must either refrain or run the risk
> of a literal (that is, a personal) interpretation. Nothing, therefore,

can prove that Shakespeare's sonnets are, or are not, autobiograph-
ical except the discovery of outside evidence that they accord, or
do not accord, with facts of his life; and no such evidence is forth-
coming. It is idle to talk of "sincerity" in this regard. Hamlet's
soliloquies are sincere, and Iago's cynical revelations of his code,
and Macbeth's poetic imaginings that visualize to the brink of
delirium. The testimony of the Sonnets must remain ambiguous.

Certainly there is much common sense in this, and many critics
have accordingly been content to view the sonnets as entirely
impersonal poetic exercises. Yet it has been pointed out also
that if Shakespeare, the greatest of dramatists, had wished to
forge a make-believe story to tie his sonnets together, he could
have created a better and more interesting one than we are
capable of finding in them.

MR. W. H.

How we approach the problem of the identity of "Mr. W.H."
depends upon how we interpret the word "begetter" in Thomas
Thorpe's enigmatic dedication. If we take it in the sense of "pro-
curer" — a sense for which we can find no other clear example
in Elizabethan literature — it must refer to the person who supplied Thorpe with his copy of the sonnets. If we take the word
in its certainly more common sense of "inspirer," it must refer
to the person to whom the poems were written. Various suggestions have been made by supporters of the first view. It has been
suggested most notably that the initials may be those of one
William Hall, an associate of Thorpe's who may have pirated
the copy for him, or those of Sir William Hervey, the third husband of Mary, Lady Southampton, mother to the young earl to
whom some scholars believe that the sonnets were written. The
assumption is that Hervey discovered the sonnets among his wife's
possessions after her death and immediately sought a printer for
them.

   Those who believe that behind the mysterious initials lies the
identity of the friend and inspirer of the poems have proposed
various candidates for the honour, but the leading contenders by
far are Henry Wriothesley, third Earl of Southampton (1573–

1620), and William Herbert, third Earl of Pembroke (1580–1630). Leslie Hotson in *Mr. W.H.* (New York: Alfred A. Knopf, 1964) has argued ingeniously that the initials are those of one William Hatcliffe, a Lincolnshire lawyer whom Shakespeare presumably met in 1587/8, when the young man was in London as a student at Gray's Inn. It is not likely, however, that Hotson's theory, which calls for the dating of the bulk of the sonnets before 1589, will dislodge Southampton or Pembroke from their long-held positions as leading contenders.

The case for Southampton is a very old one, which has been freshly argued, with considerable acerbity, by A. L. Rowse in his *William Shakespeare: A Biography* (New York: Harper and Row, 1963). It rests primarily upon the fact that Shakespeare had acknowledged Southampton as a patron in dedicating to him his *Venus and Adonis* in 1593 and *The Rape of Lucrece* in 1594, although to what extent Shakespeare actually enjoyed South-ampton's patronage is uncertain. Partisans of this theory regard the bulk of the sonnets as having been written early in Shake-speare's career. The case is further supported, somewhat dubi-ously, by the fact that W. H. are the reverse of Henry Wriothes-ley's initials (although most Southamptonites favour the notion that they are the initials of William Hervey), and by supposed allusions to Southampton's affairs in the sonnets themselves. Such personal references, it must be noted, have been adduced in sup-port of every candidate ever proposed.

Southampton, having been born in October 1573, was almost ten years younger than Shakespeare. He had been brought up in a Catholic household and retained his fidelity to the old church. On October 4, 1581, he succeeded to his father's title, and being only eight years old was made a ward of the crown and placed under the guardianship of William Cecil, Lord Burghley. In 1590, when Southampton was approaching seventeen, Burghley attempted to arrange his marriage with Lady Elizabeth Vere, the fifteen-year-old daughter of the Earl of Oxford and Burghley's own granddaughter. Southampton, however, was extraordinarily hostile to the marriage, in spite of the wishes of his mother and of the obvious advantages for a Catholic nobleman of alliance

with the powerful Vere and Cecil families. It has been suggested
that it is this particular marriage which Shakespeare is urging
upon his friend in the first seventeen sonnets, presumably having been called upon to do so by Lady Southampton. Scholars
opposed to the Southampton theory have pointed out that there
is no evidence that Shakespeare had any relations with Southampton after 1594. There seem to be no suggestion in the sonnets of the Earl's courtship of Elizabeth Vernon, which began in
1595, and which culminated in his secret marriage to her when
she became pregnant in 1598. There are no allusions to Southampton's great admiration for Essex, to the military campaigns
in which both participated, the wars in Ireland, and Essex's up-
rising, in which Southampton was involved and was sentenced
to death in 1601, although the sentence was soon changed to imprisonment, and Southampton was freed upon the accession of
King James in 1603. Unless we are to assign all of the sonnets
to an early date in Shakespeare's career, it is difficult to find in
them a great deal of pertinence to what we know about the career
of the Earl of Southampton.

The case for Pembroke has in recent times been argued most
cogently in the editions of the sonnets by O. J. Campbell and
John Dover Wilson. The son of Mary Sidney, Countess of Pembroke and nephew of Sir Philip Sidney, the third Earl of Pembroke was throughout his career, like his mother and uncle,
a patron of the arts and of poets in particular. To him, along
with his brother, the Earl of Montgomery, the First Folio of
Shakespeare's plays was dedicated in 1623. Pembroke was seven
years younger than Southampton, and those scholars who favour
his candidacy would date the bulk of the sonnets in 1597 and
1598, noting special affinities of language and theme with the
Henry IV plays, which were probably completed in 1597.

Herbert had come to court at the age of fifteen in 1595, at
which time his parents had attempted to arrange his marriage
with Lady Elizabeth Carey, granddaughter of the Lord Cham-
berlain who was the patron of Shakespeare's company. Some
scholars have seen the first seventeen sonnets as written, at the
request of either the Countess of Pembroke or the Lord Cham-

berlain, to persuade the young lord to this marriage, for which he displayed a distinct aversion. It is more likely, however, that if the sonnets do indeed refer to Pembroke, they are related to a second marriage negotiation, in the summer of 1597, when the Countess of Pembroke was attempting to affiance her son to Bridget Vere, another granddaughter of Lord Burghley. This arrangement, like the other, was never concluded, because of the young lord's strong dislike of the girl in question.

THE DARK LADY

Of the lady of the sonnets we can only say that she appears not to have been beautiful in terms of Elizabethan tastes, that she was married, and that she is unlikely to have been anyone of whom history would otherwise have left a record. Some supporters of Pembroke as the "fair youth" have attempted to identify her with Mary Fitton, a lady-in-waiting at Elizabeth's court. Her father had been close to the Sidney family, and she appears to have been befriended by the Countess of Pembroke who entertained her at Wilton, where she presumably met the young Lord Herbert who was to be her lover. After performing as a leading lady in a court masque on June 16, 1600, she came to his private chamber disguised as a boy and soon afterwards was known to be pregnant. In spite of pressure from Mary's family, Lord Herbert refused to marry her, and after the birth of her still-born child in March, 1601, he was committed to the Fleet prison by the queen. He served only a short time, being released so that he might travel abroad. Mary Fitton's later career included several rather sordid intrigues. In spite of her reputation as a loose woman, it is extremely unlikely that Shakespeare could have been involved in a liaison with a noble lady of Queen Elizabeth's court, and it has, moreover, been discovered recently that Mary Fitton was a blond. Leslie Hotson would identify the "dark lady" with one Luce Morgan, a notorious harlot who kept a brothel in Clerkenwell. The fame of her establishment was widespread, and there are various literary allusions to her darkness of complexion. If there was indeed a "dark lady," we shall probably never be certain of her identity.

THE RIVAL POET

Since both **Southampton** and **Pembroke** were famous in their day as patrons of the arts, they were courted as patrons by dozens of poets. It is thus entirely possible that Shakespeare may in different sonnets be referring to different rivals. Sonnet 76, for instance, with its reference to "new-found methods" and "compounds strange" seems to refer to the technique of the metaphysical poets, and some critics have accordingly taken the sonnet to refer to John Donne, who we know was at one time on intimate terms with Pembroke. Partisans of the Southampton school, and those generally inclined to date the sonnets early in Shakespeare's career, have suggested that the "rival poet" was Christopher Marlowe, who died in 1593. As evidence they have generally pointed to the opening line of sonnet 86: "Was it the proud full sail of his great verse." But the description would apply equally as well to the style adopted by George Chapman in his translation of the *Iliad*, the first seven books of which were published in 1598. If there was indeed a single "rival poet," most scholars today regard Chapman as the most likely possibility, although there is scarcely a poet of the age who has not at some time been suggested.

LOVE AND FRIENDSHIP

That Shakespeare should express his affection for a man in terms not unlike those used by contemporary sonneteers to praise their ladies has sometimes puzzled present-day readers, although it would not at all have puzzled Shakespeare's contemporaries. It is important that we recognize at once that there is no suggestion of homosexuality involved in the relationship, as the poet himself clearly affirms in Sonnet 20, and as is implicit in the relation of both men to the "dark lady" who has come between them. The glorification of male friendship is, in fact, a conventional upper-class affectation among Renaissance gentlemen, firmly established in the ducal courts of Italy and commonly expressed in Elizabethan literature. It may be found notably in the play *Damon and Pithias* (1571) by Richard Edwards, and in what was probably the most widely read novel of Shakespeare's day, John Lyly's *Euphues,* or *The Anatomy of Wit,* published in 1579. Friendship between men was in both of these works exalted as on a higher plane than love between man and woman. It was glorified as a more pure and disinterested passion, since, unlike a relation which could culminate in marriage, it involved complete unselfishness. The true friend gave all and expected nothing in return. It was nobler also because it existed between "equal minds," whereas woman, by her very nature, was regarded as inferior to man. Friendship was further exempt from the natural fickleness of woman (to which Shakespeare refers in Sonnet 20), and thus it was capable of a constancy and stability which no love relation between man and woman could ever really attain. Implicit in the ideal was the notion, expressed notably by Shakespeare through the story of the rings which he incorporated into *The Merchant of Venice,* that no man who did not respect the code of male friendship was really capable of loving woman. It is thus not at all to be wondered at that Shakespeare should express to the young gentleman to whom he addressed his sonnets an attitude which was a conventional part of upper-class polite affectation, and which Lyly had expressed in a prose work designed for a similar upper-class audience.

The Sonnets

TO. THE. ONLIE. BEGETTER. OF.

THESE. INSVING. SONNETS.

MR. W. H. ALL. HAPPINESSE.

AND. THAT. ETERNITIE.

PROMISED.

BY.

OVR. EVER-LIVING. POET.

WISHETH.

THE. WELL-WISHING.

ADVENTVRER. IN.

SETTING.

FORTH.

T. T.

SONNET 1.   *1 increase* progeny.   *2 rose* Not only is the rose a conventional symbol of beauty and truth, but it is commonly used in Renaissance
love poetry to stand for evanescent beauty, which is lost forever as the
petals fall.   *3 the riper . . . decease* the mature "creature" die in due
course of time.   *4 tender* young, immature.   *5 contracted* betrothed.
6 *self-substantial* composed of your own substance.   *9 ornament* that
which beautifies.   *10 only* chief.   *gaudy* gay, festive (not used in any
pejorative sense).   *11 thy content* (a) your prospects for joy (b) what you
consist of, all that you are.   *12 tender churl* dear young miser.   *mak'st
. . . niggarding* destroy (all that you consist of) by hoarding it (like a
churl or miser).   *14 the world's due* that to which the world is entitled
— propagation of the species.

SONNET 2.   *1–2 besiege thy . . . beauty's field* The metaphor is from the
practice of warfare. The "trenches" are, of course, the wrinkles of old age.
3 proud gorgeous.   *livery* outward appearance, uniform.   *4 weed* garment.   *6 lusty* full of life and spirit.   *9 deserv'd . . . use* would the
investment (use) of your beauty have deserved (since it would have
yielded you children).   *11 sum my account* pay my debt (to nature).   *make
. . . excuse* defend me against accusations (that I have wasted my beauty)
when I am old.

2

1

From fairest creatures we desire increase,
That thereby beauty's rose might never die,
But as the riper should by time decease,
His tender heir might bear his memory;
But thou, contracted to thine own bright eyes,   5
Feed'st thy light's flame with self-substantial fuel,
Making a famine where abundance lies,
Thyself thy foe, to thy sweet self too cruel.
Thou that art now the world's fresh ornament
And only herald to the gaudy spring,   10
Within thine own bud buriest thy content
And, tender churl, mak'st waste in niggarding.
  Pity the world, or else this glutton be,
  To eat the world's due, by the grave and thee.

2

When forty winters shall besiege thy brow
And dig deep trenches in thy beauty's field,
Thy youth's proud livery, so gaz'd on now,
Will be a tatter'd weed of small worth held.
Then being ask'd where all thy beauty lies,   5
Where all the treasure of thy lusty days,
To say, within thine own deep-sunken eyes
Were an all-eating shame and thriftless praise.
How much more praise deserv'd thy beauty's use
If thou couldst answer, "This fair child of mine   10
Shall sum my count and make my old excuse,"
Proving his beauty by succession thine!
  This were to be new made when thou art old
  And see thy blood warm when thou feel'st it cold.

3

SONNET 3. *3 fresh repair* youthful condition. *4 beguile* cheat. *unbless* fail to bless (some woman with motherhood). *5 unear'd* untilled. *6 husbandry* cultivation of land, farming (with a pun on "husband"). *7 fond* foolish. *tomb* monument. *8 Of his . . . posterity* to eliminate the possibility of descendants because of his own self-love. *9 thy mother's glass* the reflection of your mother's beauty. *10 Calls back* recalls. *prime* springtime, youth. *11 windows* i.e. children, through whom in your old age you will be able to see your own youth. *12 Despite* in spite. *golden time* youth. *13 But if . . . not to be* but if you live so as not to be remembered (by children). *14 image* reflection (of your beauty).

SONNET 4. *2 thy beauty's legacy* the beauty which you have inherited and should bequeath. *4 frank* generous. *are free* who are generous. *5 niggard* miser. *6 largess* generosity. *7 use* invest at interest. *8 live* (a) earn a living (b) continue to live in the memories of children. *10 deceive* cheat. *12 audit* account. *14 lives . . . to be* would live (in the form of a child) to be your executor.

4

3

Look in thy glass and tell the face thou viewest
Now is the time that face should form another,
Whose fresh repair if now thou not renewest,
Thou dost beguile the world, unbless some mother.
For where is she so fair whose unear'd womb   5
Disdains the tillage of thy husbandry?
Or who is he so fond will be the tomb
Of his self-love to stop posterity?
Thou art thy mother's glass, and she in thee
Calls back the lovely April of her prime.   10
So thou through windows of thine age shalt see,
Despite of wrinkles, this thy golden time.
    But if thou live remem'bred not to be,
    Die single, and thine image dies with thee.

4

Unthrifty loveliness, why dost thou spend
Upon thyself thy beauty's legacy?
Nature's bequest gives nothing, but doth lend,
And, being frank, she lends to those are free.
Then, beauteous niggard, why dost thou abuse   5
The bounteous largess given thee to give?
Profitless usurer, why dost thou use
So great a sum of sums, yet canst not live?
For, having traffic with thyself alone,
Thou of thyself thy sweet self dost deceive.   10
Then how, when nature calls thee to be gone,
What acceptable audit canst thou leave?
    Thy unus'd beauty must be tomb'd with thee,
    Which, used, lives th' executor to be.

5

SONNET 5. _1 frame_ shape, create. _2 The lovely . . . doth dwell_ the lovely sight upon which all eyes gaze. _4 And that . . . doth excel_ and make that unbeautiful which in beauty does excel. _6 confounds_ destroys. _him_ i.e. summer. _8 o'ersnow'd_ covered with snow. _9 summer's distillation_ perfume made from the flowers of summer. _10 pent_ locked. _11 Beauty's . . . bereft_ we would be deprived of the perfume along with the flowers from which it was made — i.e. the beauty of your unborn child as well as your beauty. _14 Leese_ lose. _their show_ their mere external appearance of physical form. _their substance_ their true spiritual essence.

SONNET 6. _1 ragged_ rough. _2 distill'd_ The image of the preceding sonnet is carried on. To be "distilled" is to be "made into perfume" — to have one's true essence carried on in the form of a child. _3 some vial_ the child into whom his essence will be distilled (not the mother). _treasure_ enrich. _5 That use_ that kind of investment (of your beauty) at interest. _6 happies_ makes happy. _7 to breed_ to give birth to. The verb "to breed" was often used to apply to the increase of capital by interest. _8 ten for one_ Ten percent was the maximum amount of interest permitted by a statute of 1571, which revived an earlier statute of Henry VIII permitting the lending of money at interest. _10 refigur'd thee_ represented thee anew as in a copy.

5

Those hours that with gentle work did frame
The lovely gaze where every eye doth dwell,
Will play the tyrants to the very same
And that unfair which fairly doth excel;
For never-resting time leads summer on   5
To hideous winter and confounds him there,
Sap check'd with frost and lusty leaves quite gone,
Beauty o'ersnow'd and bareness everywhere.
Then, were not summer's distillation left
A liquid prisoner pent in walls of glass,   10
Beauty's effect with beauty were bereft —
Nor it, nor no remembrance what it was;
    But flowers distill'd, though they with winter meet,
    Leese but their show — their substance still lives
       sweet.

6

Then let not winter's ragged hand deface
In thee thy summer ere thou be distill'd.
Make sweet some vial; treasure thou some place
With beauty's treasure ere it be self-kill'd.
That use is not forbidden usury   5
Which happies those that pay the willing loan:
That's for thyself to breed another thee,
Or ten times happier, be it ten for one.
Ten times thyself were happier than thou art,
If ten of thine ten times refigur'd thee.   10
Then what could death do if thou shouldst depart,
Leaving thee living in posterity?
    Be not self-will'd, for thou art much too fair
    To be death's conquest and make worms thine heir.

SONNET 7. *1 Orient* east. *2 under eye* eye below (on earth, as opposed to the "eye" of heaven, as the sun was conventionally called). *5 steep-up* high and precipitous. *9 highmost pitch* greatest height, i.e. noon. "Pitch" is a term from falconry indicating the greatest height to which a falcon may soar. *car* the chariot of the sun god. *11 fore* before (an old form of the word). *12 tract* track, course. *14 get* beget, conceive.

SONNET 8. The basic metaphor of the sonnet is drawn from lute playing and rests on the fact that the strings of the lute were tuned in pairs, except for the highest string, which was single. *1 Music to hear* you, whose voice is music for me to hear. *sadly* soberly, without joy. *3–4 Why lov'st . . . thine annoy* why do you either love that (music) to which you listen without joy, or tolerate at all that (music) which annoys you? If you listen to music "sadly" one of these possibilities must be true. *6 By unions married* united to one another in polyphonic combinations. *7–8 who confounds . . . shouldst bear* who destroy by singing alone the harmony of the concert (marriage) in which you should be singing only parts. The musical "parts" are the roles in the family, or "concert" of husband and father. *10 Strikes . . . ordering* To pluck one of the double strings of the lute causes the other string to vibrate as well. This is called "sympathetic vibration." *14 prove none* be no person.

8

7

Lo, in the Orient when the gracious light
Lifts up his burning head, each under eye
Doth homage to his new-appearing sight,
Serving with looks his sacred majesty;
And having climb'd the steep-up heavenly hill,   5
Resembling strong youth in his middle age,
Yet mortal looks adore his beauty still,
Attending on his golden pilgrimage;
But when from highmost pitch, with weary car,
Like feeble age he reeleth from the day,   10
The eyes (fore duteous) now converted are
From his low tract and look another way.
   So thou, thyself outgoing in thy noon,
   Unlook'd on diest unless thou get a son.

8

Music to hear, why hear'st thou music sadly?
Sweets with sweets war not, joy delights in joy.
Why lov'st thou that which thou receiv'st not gladly,
Or else receiv'st with pleasure thine annoy?
If the true concord of well-tuned sounds,   5
By unions married, do offend thine ear,
They do but sweetly chide thee, who confounds
In singleness the parts that thou shouldst bear.
Mark how one string, sweet husband to another,
Strikes each in each by mutual ordering;   10
Resembling sire and child and happy mother,
Who, all in one, one pleasing note do sing;
   Whose speechless song, being many, seeming one,
   Sings this to thee: "Thou single wilt prove none."

9

SONNET 9. *3 issueless* without children. *4 makeless* without a mate.
5 still forever. *7 private* individual (as opposed to the whole world, which
will be his "widow"). *9 Look what* whatever (a common Elizabethan
idiom). *unthrift* prodigal. *10 his* its. *11 beauty's waste* beauty wasted.
12 unus'd not permitted to reproduce itself. The metaphor is from usury.
the user he who should have "used" it. *14 murd'rous shame* shameful
murder.

SONNET 10. *6 stick'st not* do not hesitate. *7 roof* house, i.e. his friend's
body. *ruinate* ruin. *8 repair* keep in repair, maintain. *10 fairer
lodg'd* housed in a more beautiful body. *11 presence* appearance. *14
still* forever. *in thine* in your descendants.

10

9

Is it for fear to wet a widow's eye
That thou consum'st thyself in single life?
Ah! if thou issueless shalt hap to die,
The world will wail thee like a makeless wife;
The world will be thy widow, and still weep   5
That thou no form of thee hast left behind
When every private widow well may keep,
By children's eyes, her husband's shape in mind.
Look what an unthrift in the world doth spend
Shifts but his place, for still the world enjoys it;   10
But beauty's waste hath in the world an end,
And kept unus'd, the user so destroys it.
    No love toward others in that bosom sits
    That on himself such murd'rous shame commits.

10

For shame, deny that thou bear'st love to any,
Who for thyself art so unprovident.
Grant, if thou wilt, thou art belov'd of many,
But that thou none lov'st is most evident;
For thou art so possess'd with murd'rous hate   5
That 'gainst thyself thou stick'st not to conspire,
Seeking that beauteous roof to ruinate
Which to repair should be thy chief desire.
O, change thy thought, that I may change my mind!
Shall hate be fairer lodg'd than gentle love?   10
Be as thy presence is, gracious and kind,
Or to thyself at least kind-hearted prove.
    Make thee another self for love of me,
    That beauty still may live in thine or thee.

SONNET 11. *1–2 As fast . . . thou departest* as fast as you decline (in old age) so fast shall you grow, in the form of your child, toward the peak (of youthful beauty) from which you are declining. *3 which . . . bestow'st* which while you are young you put out to gain interest. *4 convertest* turn away. *5 Herein* by this course of action. *7 the times* the succeeding generations of men. *9 store* breeding, replenishment. *10 barrenly* without children. *11 Look whom* whomever (a common Elizabethan idiom). *12 bounteous gift* (a) generous gift (b) gift of bounty, of ability to procreate. *in bounty* by being prolific. *13 seal* engraved stamp used to make impressions in wax. *14 copy* original, archetype, from which copies are made (as in "printer's copy").

SONNET 12. *1 count the clock* count the hours as they are struck by the clock. *tells* (a) reveals (b) counts. *2 brave* magnificent, radiant. *3 past prime* faded. *4 sable* black. *all* MALONE; Q: "or." *6 erst* formerly. *7 summer's green* i.e. the grain, which is conceived of as born on the harvest carts in bound-up sheaves like dead men being carried to their graves. *8 bristly beard* This may suggest barley. *9 question make* consider, speculate about. *10 the wastes of time* those things which time destroys. *11 themselves forsake* cease to be what they formerly were, deteriorate with time. *12 others* other "sweets and beauties." *13 Time's scythe* The conventional symbol of Time with his scythe supports and echoes the reaping image of lines 7–8. *14 breed* children. *brave* defy.

12

As fast as thou shalt wane, so fast thou grow'st
In one of thine, from that which thou departest;
And that fresh blood which youngly thou bestow'st
Thou mayst call thine when thou from youth con-
    vertest.
Herein lives wisdom, beauty, and increase;   5
Without this, folly, age, and cold decay.
If all were minded so, the times should cease,
And threescore year would make the world away.
Let those whom Nature hath not made for store,
Harsh, featureless, and rude, barrenly perish.   10
Look whom she best endow'd she gave the more,
Which bounteous gift thou shouldst in bounty cherish.
    She carv'd thee for her seal, and meant thereby
    Thou shouldst print more, not let that copy die.

When I do count the clock that tells the time
And see the brave day sunk in hideous night,
When I behold the violet past prime
And sable curls all silver'd o'er with white,
When lofty trees I see barren of leaves,   5
Which erst from heat did canopy the herd,
And summer's green all girded up in sheaves
Borne on the bier with white and bristly beard —
Then of thy beauty do I question make
That thou among the wastes of time must go,   10
Since sweets and beauties do themselves forsake
And die as fast as they see others grow,
    And nothing 'gainst Time's scythe can make defence
    Save breed, to brave him when he takes thee hence.

SONNET 13. *1 O, that . . . yourself* O, that your present self could be your eternal self. The opening sentence deliberately shocks the reader by its ambiguity, and the rest of the sonnet serves to explain it. *1–2 you are . . . here live* you retain your present form only so long as you remain alive. *3 Against* in anticipation of. *5 in lease* for a short time only. Man can only lease his body; he cannot own it since it must be taken away from him by death. *6 determination* ending (a legal term). *you were* you would be. *7 Yourself* MALONE; Q: "You selfe." *8 issue* offspring. *10 husbandry* (a) prudent management (b) tillage (c) assuming the role of husband. *in honour* in marriage. *12 barren rage of* fruitless ravaging by. *13 unthrifts* prodigals.

SONNET 14. *1 pluck* derive. *2 have* understand. *astronomy* ability to foretell the future by means of the stars. There was no distinction in Shakespeare's day between astronomy and astrology. *3–4 of good . . . seasons' quality* These were the traditional subjects of astrologers. *5 to brief minutes* down to the smallest details, covering the shortest periods of time. *6 Pointing to each* assigning to each minute. *his* its. *8 oft predict that* often predicting what. *10 read such art* gather such knowledge. *12 store* fertility. *convert* turn. *14 Thy end . . . and date* your death will also mark the prescribed end of truth and beauty.

14

13

O, that you were yourself! but, love, you are
No longer yours than you yourself here live.
Against this coming end you should prepare
And your sweet semblance to some other give.
So should that beauty which you hold in lease   5
Find no determination; then you were
Yourself again after yourself's decease
When your sweet issue your sweet form should bear.
Who lets so fair a house fall to decay,
Which husbandry in honour might uphold   10
Against the stormy gusts of winter's day
And barren rage of death's eternal cold?
   O, none but unthrifts! Dear my love, you know
   You had a father — let your son say so.

14

Not from the stars do I my judgment pluck,
And yet methinks I have astronomy;
But not to tell of good or evil luck,
Of plagues, of dearths, or seasons' quality;
Nor can I fortune to brief minutes tell,   5
Pointing to each his thunder, rain, and wind,
Or say with princes if it shall go well
By oft predict that I in heaven find;
But from thine eyes my knowledge I derive,
And, constant stars, in them I read such art   10
As truth and beauty shall together thrive
If from thyself to store thou wouldst convert;
   Or else of thee this I prognosticate:
   Thy end is truth's and beauty's doom and date.

15

SONNET 15. *1 consider* consider that. *2 Holds* endures. *3 huge stage* the world (which Shakespeare often conceives of in terms of the theatre). *shows* insubstantial external appearances. *4 Whereon . . . comment* The stars are conceived of as influencing the course of human events in the same way that the audience may comment upon the performance of players on a stage, but while the audience reacts noisily, the stars comment in silence. "Influence" is a technical term in astrology for the power exerted by a star. *6 Cheered* encouraged. *check'd* (a) rebuked (b) restrained. *7 Vaunt* boast, exult and swagger. *sap* vigour. *8 wear . . . memory* wear away their magnificent condition (as a garment is worn out) until it is forgotten. *9 conceit* thought. *inconstant stay* impermanent condition of life. *11 debateth with* contends in rivalry with. *14 ingraft you* give you new life (by means of my poetry) as trees are revivified by grafting. Here the poet introduces a new theme: the power of his poetry to keep his friend's beauty alive after it has faded.

SONNET 16. *1 a mightier way* mightier than by the poet's pen. *3 fortify* repair. *4 barren rhyme* The poem can produce no children, whereas the "mightier way" can produce a son. Shakespeare is not simply depreciating his own verse. *5 on the . . . hours* at the prime of life. *6 yet unset* still unseeded. *8 Much liker . . . counterfeit* resembling you more closely than your portrait can. *9 lines of life* lineal descendants. *life repair* restore life (through children after life in the parent is gone). *10 pencil* the painter's brush. *pupil* inexperienced, still learning. Some have taken this as evidence that the sonnet is one of Shakespeare's earliest. *13 give away yourself* get married. *14 drawn* sketched, described. The friend himself, by his own marriage, must replace the inadequate efforts of the artist and the poet.

16

When I consider every thing that grows
Holds in perfection but a little moment,
That this huge stage presenteth naught but shows
Whereon the stars in secret influence comment;
When I perceive that men as plants increase,   5
Cheered and check'd even by the selfsame sky,
Vaunt in their youthful sap, at height decrease,
And wear their brave state out of memory:
Then the conceit of this inconstant stay
Sets you most rich in youth before my sight,   10
Where wasteful Time debateth with Decay
To change your day of youth to sullied night
    And, all in war with Time for love of you,
    As he takes from you, I ingraft you new.

But wherefore do not you a mightier way
Make war upon this bloody tyrant, Time?
And fortify yourself in your decay
With means more blessed than my barren rhyme?
Now stand you on the top of happy hours;   5
And many maiden gardens, yet unset,
With virtuous wish would bear your living flowers,
Much liker than your painted counterfeit.
So should the lines of life that life repair
Which this time's pencil, or my pupil pen,   10
Neither in inward worth nor outward fair
Can make you live yourself in eyes of men.
    To give away yourself keeps yourself still,
    And you must live, drawn by your own sweet skill.

SONNET 17. *2 were fill'd with* fully expressed. *deserts* merits. *4 parts* qualities, endowments. *6 fresh* lively. *numbers* verses. *8 touches* Either (a) attributes, traits or (b) brush strokes. *11 rage* wild inspiration (and therefore irrational and false). *12 stretched* exaggerated. *antique* quaint and old.

SONNET 18. *2 temperate* even-tempered, mild. *3 May* In Shakespeare's calendar May would extend into what in our calendar is the middle of June. *4 date* duration. *5 eye of heaven* sun. *6 dimm'd* covered with clouds. *7 every fair . . . declines* every beautiful object must at some time cease to be beautiful. *8 untrimm'd* stripped of its beautiful ornamentation. *10 fair* beauty. *thou ow'st* which you possess. *11 shade* place of oblivion. *12 to . . . grow'st* become a part of time, are grafted to time, as a shoot becomes part of the tree to which it is grafted. *14 this* i.e. the poem.

18

17

Who will believe my verse in time to come
If it were fill'd with your most high deserts?
Though yet, heaven knows, it is but as a tomb
Which hides your life and shows not half your parts.
If I could write the beauty of your eyes   5
And in fresh numbers number all your graces,
The age to come would say, "This poet lies!
Such heavenly touches ne'er touch'd earthly faces."
So should my papers (yellowed with their age)
Be scorn'd, like old men of less truth than tongue,   10
And your true rights be term'd a poet's rage
And stretched metre of an antique song.
    But were some child of yours alive that time,
    You should live twice — in it, and in my rhyme.

18

Shall I compare thee to a summer's day?
Thou art more lovely and more temperate.
Rough winds do shake the darling buds of May,
And summer's lease hath all too short a date.
Sometime too hot the eye of heaven shines,   5
And often is his gold complexion dimm'd;
And every fair from fair sometime declines,
By chance, or nature's changing course, untrimm'd;
But thy eternal summer shall not fade
Nor lose possession of that fair thou ow'st,   10
Nor shall Death brag thou wand'rest in his shade
When in eternal lines to time thou grow'st.
    So long as men can breathe or eyes can see,
    So long lives this, and this gives life to thee.

SONNET 19. *2 devour . . . brood* take back within herself the beautiful things (here primarily the flowers) which have sprung from her.   *4 phœnix* a mythical bird which, after having lived for many centuries, bursts into fire and is reborn out of its own ashes. It was a conventional symbol of immortality. *in her blood* alive.   *5 fleets* DYCE; Q: "fleet'st." Both were common Elizabethan forms.   *10 antique* (a) ancient (b) antic, grotesque.   *11 untainted* (a) untouched, unsullied (b) uninjured. To "taint" was to "hit" in the sport of tilting.   *12 beauty's . . . men* a model of perfect beauty to be admired by succeeding generations.   *13 wrong* injury.

SONNET 20. In this sonnet the poet affirms the masculinity of his friend and disclaims any homosexual interest on his own part.   *1 with Nature's . . . painted* of natural beauty, not aided by cosmetics.   *2 master mistress* mistress who is a man (as opposed to the female mistresses of other sonnet writers). The point is that his friend's beauty is causing the poet to address him as other poets address their mistresses, but he is, in fact, a man and the poet's master. *passion* love.   *5 rolling* passing from one object to another.   *6 Gilding* The metaphor rests upon the notion that the eye exuded beams upon objects in its sight. Like the sun, his friend's eye gives forth beams of gold.   *7 A man . . . his* controlling a man whose form (hue) may set the standard by which the forms of other men may be judged. By "hue" is meant the peculiar combination of humours within the body which was believed to determine the total human being, both in physique and personality.   *8 Which* who.   *11 defeated* defrauded.   *12 to my . . . nothing* of no use to me.   *13 prick'd thee out* selected you especially (with the obvious quibble).   *14 use* employment for sexual purposes.

19

Devouring Time, blunt thou the lion's paws
And make the earth devour her own sweet brood;
Pluck the keen teeth from the fierce tiger's jaws
And burn the long-liv'd phœnix in her blood;
Make glad and sorry seasons as thou fleets,   5
And do whate'er thou wilt, swift-footed Time,
To the wide world and all her fading sweets;
But I forbid thee one most heinous crime:
O, carve not with thy hours my love's fair brow,
Nor draw no lines there with thine antique pen!   10
Him in thy course untainted do allow
For beauty's pattern to succeeding men.
　　Yet do thy worst, old Time! Despite thy wrong,
　　My love shall in my verse ever live young.

20

A woman's face, with Nature's own hand painted,
Hast thou, the master mistress of my passion;
A woman's gentle heart, but not acquainted
With shifting change, as is false women's fashion;
An eye more bright than theirs, less false in rolling,   5
Gilding the object whereupon it gazeth;
A man in hue all hues in his controlling,
Which steals men's eyes and women's souls amazeth.
And for a woman wert thou first created,
Till Nature as she wrought thee fell a-doting   10
And by addition me of thee defeated
By adding one thing to my purpose nothing.
　　But since she prick'd thee out for women's pleasure,
　　Mine be thy love, and thy love's use their treasure.

SONNET 21. In this sonnet the "rival poet" makes his first appearance. Shakespeare compares his own simple style with the ornate and extravagant manner of the poet he is mocking. *1 Muse* poet. *2 Stirr'd* inspired. *painted* artificial (as opposed to the "natural" beauty of Shakespeare's inspiration). *4 every fair . . . rehearse* mentions every beautiful thing in the world in comparison with the beauty he is praising. *5 couplement* combination. *compare* comparison. *8 in this . . . hems* that is enclosed within this sphere of earth (encircled by the dome of the sky). *12 candles* stars. *13 that like . . . well* who are fond of exaggerated, secondhand comparisons. *14 purpose not to sell* am not a merchant. Merchants, of course, proverbially overpraise their wares.

SONNET 22. The sonnet embodies the Renaissance convention that lovers have exchanged hearts. *1 glass* mirror. *old* It was conventional since the time of Petrarch for sonneteers to claim old age. *2 So long . . . one date* so long as you are young. *4 expiate* finish, wind up. *6 seemly raiment* beautiful covering. *11 keep so chary* guard so carefully. *13 Presume not on* do not expect to get back.

So is it not with me as with that Muse
Stirr'd by a painted beauty to his verse,
Who heaven itself for ornament doth use
And every fair with his fair doth rehearse;
Making a couplement of proud compare   5
With sun and moon, with earth and sea's rich gems,
With April's first-born flowers, and all things rare
That heaven's air in this huge rondure hems.
O, let me, true in love, but truly write,
And then believe me, my love is as fair   10
As any mother's child, though not so bright
As those gold candles fix'd in heaven's air.
    Let them say more that like of hearsay well;
    I will not praise that purpose not to sell.

My glass shall not persuade me I am old
So long as youth and thou are of one date;
But when in thee time's furrows I behold,
Then look I death my days should expiate.
For all that beauty that doth cover thee   5
Is but the seemly raiment of my heart,
Which in thy breast doth live, as thine in me.
How can I then be elder than thou art?
O, therefore, love, be of thyself so wary
As I, not for myself, but for thee will,   10
Bearing thy heart, which I will keep so chary
As tender nurse her babe from faring ill.
    Presume not on thy heart when mine is slain:
    Thou gav'st me thine, not to give back again.

23

SONNET 23. *1 an unperfect actor* an actor who has not yet learned his part. *2 with* by. *besides* out of. *3–4 Or some . . . own heart* or like a savage beast who finds that his passion by its very intensity makes him incapable of expressing it. *5 for fear of trust* afraid of overconfidence, of trusting too much in my own ability. *6 perfect . . . rite* exact words appropriate to love's ritual. *7 decay* weaken, falter. *9 looks* CAPELL; Q: "books." *10 dumb presagers* His looks are likened to the dumb shows which often preceded the dialogue in old plays. They were pantomime enactments of the coming scene. *12 that tongue* i.e. of the "rival poet." *that more . . . more express'd* that more fully has expressed more of your perfections. *14 belongs . . . wit* is a characteristic of love's fine powers of perception.

SONNET 24. *1 stell'd* fixed (CAPELL; Q: "steeld," which is retained by some editors as meaning "engraved"). *2 table* board on which a picture was painted. *4 perspective* (a) when seen from the proper angle (b) when seen as through a perspective glass. The word is accented on the first syllable. *7 shop* workshop, studio. *8 his* its. *glazed* covered with glass. *13 this cunning want* lack this skill. *grace* enhance.

✧✧✧✧✧✧✧✧✧ 23

As an unperfect actor on the stage
Who with his fear is put besides his part,
Or some fierce thing replete with too much rage,
Whose strength's abundance weakens his own heart;
So I, for fear of trust, forget to say   5
The perfect ceremony of love's rite,
And in mine own love's strength seem to decay,
O'ercharg'd with burden of mine own love's might.
O, let my looks be then the eloquence
And dumb presagers of my speaking breast,   10
Who plead for love, and look for recompense,
More than that tongue that more hath more express'd.
    O, learn to read what silent love hath writ!
    To hear with eyes belongs to love's fine wit.

✧✧✧✧✧✧✧✧✧ 24

Mine eye hath play'd the painter and hath stell'd
Thy beauty's form in table of my heart;
My body is the frame wherein 'tis held,
And perspective it is best painter's art.
For through the painter must you see his skill   5
To find where your true image pictur'd lies,
Which in my bosom's shop is hanging still,
That hath his windows glazed with thine eyes.
Now see what good turns eyes for eyes have done:
Mine eyes have drawn thy shape, and thine for me   10
Are windows to my breast, wherethrough the sun
Delights to peep, to gaze therein on thee.
    Yet eyes this cunning want to grace their art —
    They draw but what they see, know not the heart.

SONNET 25. *1 who are . . . their stars* who are favoured by their stars (which were believed to determine human destiny). *3 whom . . . bars* A probable reference to Shakespeare's lowly station as a player. *4 Unlook'd for* unexpectedly. *that* what. *6 marigold* The English marigold (Calendula officinalis) closed at sunset. *9 painful* toiling. *famoused* famous. *fight* THEOBALD; Q: "worth." *10 foil'd* defeated in battle. *11 rased quite* erased entirely. *14 I may . . . be removed* I may not cease to love or to be loved.

SONNET 26. This sonnet is a formal letter in which the poet addresses his friend as a vassal might address his lord. Some suspect that it was written to accompany the gift of the preceding sonnets. *3 embassage* message delivered by an ambassador (Q: "ambassage"). *4 witness* give evidence of. *wit* skill. *7 good conceit* favourable opinion. *8 In thy . . . bestow it* will receive it to your heart despite its nakedness. *9 moving* existence. *10 Points on* sheds beams upon. *fair aspect* favourable influence. The "aspect" of a star was an astrological term for the "influence" it exerted on human affairs. *12 of thy* CAPELL; Q: "of their." *14 prove* test.

26

25

Let those who are in favour with their stars
Of public honour and proud titles boast,
Whilst I, whom fortune of such triumph bars,
Unlook'd for joy in that I honour most.
Great princes' favourites their fair leaves spread   5
But as the marigold at the sun's eye;
And in themselves their pride lies buried,
For at a frown they in their glory die.
The painful warrior famoused for fight,
After a thousand victories once foil'd,   10
Is from the book of honour rased quite,
And all the rest forgot for which he toil'd.
    Then happy I, that love and am beloved
    Where I may not remove nor be removed.

26

Lord of my love, to whom in vassalage
Thy merit hath my duty strongly knit,
To thee I send this written embassage,
To witness duty, not to show my wit:
Duty so great, which wit so poor as mine   5
May make seem bare, in wanting words to show it,
But that I hope some good conceit of thine
In thy soul's thought (all naked) will bestow it;
Till whatsoever star that guides my moving
Points on me graciously with fair aspect,   10
And puts apparel on my tattered loving
To show me worthy of thy sweet respect.
    Then may I dare to boast how I do love thee;
    Till then not show my head where thou mayst prove
      me.

SONNETS 27–28. These sonnets, expressing the poet's sorrow at separation from his friend, were probably written while Shakespeare was on a tour of the provinces with his company.

SONNET 27. *2 travel* (a) labour (b) travel. *4 work my mind* keep my thoughts active. *6 Intend* set out upon. *pilgrimage* The lover as a pilgrim and his beloved as a saint was a common metaphor of Renaissance love poetry. *9 imaginary* existing only in imagination. *10 thy* CAPELL; Q: "their." *shadow* apparition. *13–14 by day . . . quiet find* by day my limbs are tired by my journey, and by night I cannot rest because of your image in my mind.

SONNET 28. *3 oppression* distress. *5 either's* each other's. *6 shake hands* ratify their agreement. *7 to complain* by causing me to complain. *8 How far I toil* no matter how far I travel. *10 dost him grace* confer beauty upon him (the day). *11 flatter* beguile. *swart-complexion'd* composed of blackness. *12 twire* peep, twinkle. *gild'st the even* make the evening shine like gold. *13 draw* draw out, prolong. *14 strength* DYCE; Q: "length."

28

Weary with toil, I haste me to my bed,
The dear repose for limbs with travel tired;
But then begins a journey in my head
To work my mind when body's work's expired.
For then my thoughts, from far where I abide, 5
Intend a zealous pilgrimage to thee,
And keep my drooping eyelids open wide,
Looking on darkness which the blind do see;
Save that my soul's imaginary sight
Presents thy shadow to my sightless view, 10
Which, like a jewel hung in ghastly night,
Makes black night beauteous and her old face new.
Lo, thus, by day my limbs, by night my mind,
For thee, and for myself, no quiet find.

How can I then return in happy plight
That am debarr'd the benefit of rest,
When day's oppression is not eas'd by night,
But day by night and night by day oppress'd,
And each, though enemies to either's reign, 5
Do in consent shake hands to torture me,
The one by toil, the other to complain
How far I toil, still farther off from thee?
I tell the day, to please him, thou art bright
And dost him grace when clouds do blot the heaven; 10
So flatter I the swart-complexion'd night,
When sparkling stars twire not, thou gild'st the even.
But day doth daily draw my sorrows longer,
And night doth nightly make grief's strength seem
stronger.

SONNET 29. *1 in disgrace* out of favour. *2 outcast state* referring probably to his position as a common actor. *3 bootless* futile. *5 more rich
in hope* with greater expectations. *6 like him, like him* like one man,
like another man. *7 art* skill or learning. *scope* intellectual range. *8
most enjoy* possess in the highest degree. He probably means his poetic
talent. *10 Haply* by chance. *state* state of mind. *12 sullen* gloomy,
dark.

SONNET 30. *1-2 When to . . . things past* Thought is conceived of as a
court of law (sessions) before which past memories are summoned to
render their account. *3 sigh* lament. *4 with old . . . time's waste* in
recalling ancient sorrows (or in addition to them) I weep anew for the
wasting of my precious time. *6 dateless* without termination. *7 And
weep . . . cancell'd woe* and by freshly weeping pay again the debt of
sorrow (for unrequited love) which has long ago been paid in full. *8
expense* loss. *9 foregone* already past and done with. *10 heavily* sadly.
tell count.

30

When, in disgrace with Fortune and men's eyes,
I all alone beweep my outcast state,
And trouble deaf heaven with my bootless cries,
And look upon myself and curse my fate,
Wishing me like to one more rich in hope,   5
Featur'd like him, like him with friends possess'd,
Desiring this man's art, and that man's scope,
With what I most enjoy contented least;
Yet in these thoughts myself almost despising,
Haply I think on thee, and then my state,   10
Like to the lark at break of day arising
From sullen earth, sings hymns at heaven's gate;
   For thy sweet love rememb'red such wealth brings
   That then I scorn to change my state with kings.

When to the sessions of sweet silent thought
I summon up remembrance of things past,
I sigh the lack of many a thing I sought
And with old woes new wail my dear time's waste.
Then can I drown an eye (unus'd to flow)   5
For precious friends hid in death's dateless night,
And weep afresh love's long since cancell'd woe,
And moan th' expense of many a vanish'd sight.
Then can I grieve at grievances foregone,
And heavily from woe to woe tell o'er   10
The sad account of fore-bemoaned moan,
Which I new pay as if not paid before.
   But if the while I think on thee, dear friend,
   All losses are restor'd and sorrows end.

SONNET 31. The point of the sonnet is that all of the poet's past friends, supposedly dead, are enshrined in his living friend. *1 endeared with* made more precious by. *3 parts* qualities, attributes. *5 obsequious* shed in mourning. *6 religious* faithful. *7 interest* a right or claim. *appear* are revealed to be. *8 But things remov'd* merely absent things. *thee* GILDON; Q: "there." *10 trophies* memorials, such as were hung on tombstones to honour the dead. *lovers* friends. *11 parts* shares. *12 due of many* what was formerly due to many. *14 all they* who unite all of them in yourself. *all the all* the sum total (of all my parts).

SONNET 32. *1 my well-contented day* the day (of my death) which I will be pleased to see. *2 churl* rude country fellow. Death is envisioned as a gravedigger. *3 by fortune* by chance. *4 poor rude lines* That Shakespeare should appear to deprecate his own verse is entirely in accord with Renaissance custom. *lover* friend. *5 bett'ring of the time* improvement being made in the poetry of this age. *7 Reserve* preserve. *rhyme* excellence as poetry. *8 happier* more fortunate (in having greater poetic gifts). *10 grown . . . age* improved as the poetry of this age has improved. *12 in ranks . . . equipage* in the company of poets of superior style. "Equipage" is literally "military equipment." *13 better prove* turn out to be better. *14 Theirs* their poems.

32

31

Thy bosom is endeared with all hearts
Which I by lacking have supposed dead;
And there reigns love, and all love's loving parts,
And all those friends which I thought buried.
How many a holy and obsequious tear   5
Hath dear religious love stol'n from mine eye,
As interest of the dead, which now appear
But things remov'd that hidden in thee lie!
Thou art the grave where buried love doth live,
Hung with the trophies of my lovers gone,   10
Who all their parts of me to thee did give:
That due of many now is thine alone.
   Their images I lov'd I view in thee,
   And thou (all they) hast all the all of me.

32

If thou survive my well-contented day
When that churl Death my bones with dust shall cover,
And shalt by fortune once more resurvey
These poor rude lines of thy deceased lover,
Compare them with the bett'ring of the time,   5
And though they be outstripp'd by every pen,
Reserve them for my love not for their rhyme,
Exceeded by the height of happier men.
O, then vouchsafe me but this loving thought:
"Had my friend's Muse grown with this growing age,   10
A dearer birth than this his love had brought,
To march in ranks of better equipage;
   But since he died, and poets better prove,
   Theirs for their style I'll read, his for his love."

SONNET 33. *2 Flatter . . . eye* The sun flatters the mountaintop on which it shines just as the king flatters the subject upon whom he looks. The sun-king analogy is traditional. *5 basest* darkest. *6 rack* mass of drifting clouds. *8 disgrace* blemish, disfigurement. *12 region cloud* the "rack" of clouds of the upper air. *13 no whit* not at all. *14 stain* grow dim, lose their brightness.

SONNET 34. *3 base* dark. *4 brav'ry* splendour. *rotten smoke* unwholesome fog (commonly believed to carry the plague). *6 the rain* i.e. my tears. *8 disgrace* blemish, scar. *9 give physic to* cure. *12 cross* frustrating burden (CAPELL; Q: "losse"). *13 sheeds* sheds. The Q spelling is preserved for the sake of rhyme. *14 ransom* atone for.

33

Full many a glorious morning have I seen
Flatter the mountain tops with sovereign eye,
Kissing with golden face the meadows green,
Gilding pale streams with heavenly alchemy;
Anon permit the basest clouds to ride   5
With ugly rack on his celestial face
And from the forlorn world his visage hide,
Stealing unseen to West with this disgrace.
Even so my sun one early morn did shine
With all triumphant splendour on my brow;   10
But, out alack! he was but one hour mine,
The region cloud hath mask'd him from me now.
   Yet him for this my love no whit disdaineth;
    Suns of the world may stain when heaven's sun
      staineth.

34

Why didst thou promise such a beauteous day
And make me travel forth without my cloak,
To let base clouds o'ertake me in my way,
Hiding thy brav'ry in their rotten smoke?
'Tis not enough that through the cloud thou break   5
To dry the rain on my storm-beaten face,
For no man well of such a salve can speak
That heals the wound, and cures not the disgrace:
Nor can thy shame give physic to my grief;
Though thou repent, yet I have still the loss.   10
Th' offender's sorrow lends but weak relief
To him that bears the strong offence's cross.
   Ah, but those tears are pearl which thy love sheeds,
    And they are rich and ransom all ill deeds.

35

SONNET 35. *3 stain* darken. *4 canker* a green caterpillar which feeds upon blossoms. *5 make faults* have their faults. *6 Authorizing* justifying. *with compare* by comparison. *7 salving thy amiss* in palliating your offence. *8 Excusing . . . sins are* offering excuses for your sins (so anxious am I to forgive you) that are greater than your sins would call for. *thy . . . thy* CAPELL; Q: "their . . . their." *9 sense* (a) reason, rationalization (b) feeling, sympathetic understanding. There is a probable pun on "incense." *10 Thy adverse . . . advocate* the one you have injured pleads for you. *13 accessary* accomplice. *14 sourly* bitterly.

SONNET 36. *1 twain* separated. *3 blots* defects. He may be referring to the corruption he has himself suffered because of his friend's disloyalty. *5 one respect* a single attitude. *6 a separable spite* a spiteful (cruel) situation which separates us. *7 love's sole effect* the emotions to which only love can give rise. *9 not evermore* no longer. *acknowledge thee* give signs that I know thee (when we meet). *10 bewailed* lamented. *guilt* To just what guilt the poet is referring is not clear. It may be the "blots" of line 3, or perhaps his relations with the "dark lady." *11 public kindness* public recognition by a nobleman. *12 Unless . . . name* unless you wish to dishonour yourself by so doing. *14 mine . . . report* your good reputation is in my keeping. Shakespeare uses this same couplet to conclude Sonnet 96.

35

No more be griev'd at that which thou hast done:
Roses have thorns, and silver fountains mud;
Clouds and eclipses stain both moon and sun,
And loathsome canker lives in sweetest bud.
All men make faults, and even I in this,   5
Authorizing thy trespass with compare,
Myself corrupting, salving thy amiss,
Excusing thy sins more than thy sins are;
For to thy sensual fault I bring in sense —
Thy adverse party is thy advocate —   10
And 'gainst myself a lawful plea commence.
Such civil war is in my love and hate
    That I an accessary needs must be
    To that sweet thief which sourly robs from me.

36

Let me confess that we two must be twain,
Although our undivided loves are one.
So shall those blots that do with me remain,
Without thy help by me be borne alone.
In our two loves there is but one respect,   5
Though in our lives a separable spite,
Which though it alter not love's sole effect,
Yet doth it steal sweet hours from love's delight.
I may not evermore acknowledge thee,
Lest my bewailed guilt should do thee shame;   10
Nor thou with public kindness honour me,
Unless thou take that honour from thy name.
    But do not so. I love thee in such sort
    As, thou being mine, mine is thy good report.

SONNET 37. *3 made lame* handicapped. We are not to conclude, as some have done, that the poet is referring to a specific physical defect. *dearest* direst, most grievous. *4 worth* nobility. *7 Entitled . . . sit* sit crowned among your virtuous qualities (parts). *thy* CAPELL; Q: "their." *8 engrafted to this store* fastened to and drawing sustenance from this abundance (of your "parts"), as a shoot is grafted to the trunk of a tree. *10 Whilst that . . . substance give* while this idea of mine (that I share in your "parts") enables me to share in their actuality. "Shadow" and "substance" are often contrasted in Elizabethan philosophy. *11 suffic'd* satisfied, contented. *12 And by . . . live* The poet lives by his love for his friend, and that love is itself a part of the glory which his friend possesses. *13 Look what* whatever.

SONNET 38. *1 subject to invent* subject matter for poetry. "Invention" is "poetic creativity." *3 argument* theme. *4 For every . . . rehearse* for any common piece of writing to express. *5–6 if aught . . . thy sight* if anything I have written which is worth the reading meets your eye. *10 invocate* invoke, call upon for inspiration. *12 numbers* verses. *date* periods of time. *13 these curious days* this highly critical age. *14 pain* effort, trouble.

37

As a decrepit father takes delight
To see his active child do deeds of youth,
So I, made lame by Fortune's dearest spite,
Take all my comfort of thy worth and truth;
For whether beauty, birth, or wealth, or wit,   5
Or any of these all, or all, or more,
Entitled in thy parts do crowned sit,
I make my love engrafted to this store.
So then I am not lame, poor, nor despis'd
Whilst that this shadow doth such substance give   10
That I in thy abundance am suffic'd
And by a part of all thy glory live.
    Look what is best — that best I wish in thee.
    This wish I have; then ten times happy me!

38

How can my Muse want subject to invent
While thou dost breathe, that pour'st into my verse
Thine own sweet argument, too excellent
For every vulgar paper to rehearse?
O, give thyself the thanks if aught in me   5
Worthy perusal stand against thy sight;
For who's so dumb that cannot write to thee,
When thou thyself dost give invention light?
Be thou the tenth Muse, ten times more in worth
Than those old nine which rhymers invoke;   10
And he that calls on thee, let him bring forth
Eternal numbers to outlive long date.
    If my slight Muse do please these curious days,
    The pain be mine, but thine shall be the praise.

SONNET 39. *1 with manners* with decent modesty (since it is not modest to praise oneself). *2 the better part of me* my soul. *5 for* because of. *6 name* report (as opposed to the reality). *8 That due* that which is owed. *9 absence* separation. *prove* prove to be. *11 entertain* pass pleasantly. *12 doth* MALONE; Q: "dost." *deceive* beguile. *13 to make one twain* to make one person appear to be two. Absence of his friend causes the poet to envision him in his imagination and thus add his friend's presence to his own. *14 hence* away from here.

SONNET 40. *1 Take all . . . them all* take all the kinds of love I have: (a) my love for you (b) my mistress whom I love. *3–4 No love . . . this more* the love of my mistress cannot be called true love, and all my love for you was already yours before you took my mistress. *5 for my love* (a) because of love for me, since you must love anything that belongs to me (b) in exchange for my love for you (c) because of my love for her. *thou . . . receivest* you take my mistress. *6 for* because. *usest* employ for sexual purposes. *7 thyself* MALONE; Q: "this selfe." *deceivest* betray, are false to. *8 wilful taste* (a) lustful savouring (b) deliberate enjoyment. *thyself refusest* your better nature would reject. *10 all my poverty* all the little I possess. *12 hate's known injury* that kind of injury of which we know hatred to be capable. *13 Lascivious grace* beauty and charm in lustfulness. *14 spites* outrageous injuries.

40

39

O, how thy worth with manners may I sing
When thou art all the better part of me?
What can mine own praise to mine own self bring?
And what is't but mine own when I praise thee?
Even for this let us divided live   5
And our dear love lose name of single one,
That by this separation I may give
That due to thee which thou deserv'st alone.
O absence, what a torment wouldst thou prove,
Were it not thy sour leisure gave sweet leave   10
To entertain the time with thoughts of love,
Which time and thoughts so sweetly doth deceive,
   And that thou teachest how to make one twain —
   By praising him here who doth hence remain!

40

Take all my loves, my love, yea, take them all!
What hast thou then more than thou hadst before?
No love, my love, that thou mayst true love call;
All mine was thine before thou hadst this more.
Then, if for my love thou my love receivest,   5
I cannot blame thee for my love thou usest;
But yet be blam'd if thou thyself deceivest
By wilful taste of what thyself refusest.
I do forgive thy robb'ry, gentle thief,
Although thou steal thee all my poverty;   10
And yet love knows it is a greater grief
To bear love's wrong than hate's known injury.
   Lascivious grace, in whom all ill well shows,
   Kill me with spites; yet we must not be foes.

SONNET 41. *1 pretty wrongs* (a) slight misdeeds (b) misdeeds graciously committed — the "Lascivious grace" of the previous sonnet. *liberty* lust. *4 still* always. *8 sourly* rudely. *she* MALONE; Q: "he." *9 my seat forbear* forgo the special position that belongs to me — i.e. not take my place with my mistress. *10 chide* rebuke. *straying* moving from object to object. *11 riot* debauchery. *12 a twofold truth* the faith (troth) of the mistress to the poet and that of the friend to the poet.

SONNET 42. *3 of my wailing chief* my chief cause of lamentation. *7 abuse* deceive. *8 Suff'ring* permitting. *approve her* (a) think well of her (b) put her to the test, try her out. *9 my love's* my mistress's. *10 losing her* if I lose her. *11 both twain* both of them. *12 cross* affliction. *14 Sweet flattery* pleasing self-deception.

42

Those pretty wrongs that liberty commits
When I am sometime absent from thy heart,
Thy beauty and thy years full well befits,
For still temptation follows where thou art.
Gentle thou art, and therefore to be won;　　　5
Beauteous thou art, therefore to be assailed;
And when a woman woos, what woman's son
Will sourly leave her till she have prevailed?
Ay me! but yet thou mightst my seat forbear,
And chide thy beauty and thy straying youth,　　10
Who lead thee in their riot even there
Where thou art forc'd to break a twofold truth —
　　Hers, by thy beauty tempting her to thee,
　　Thine, by thy beauty being false to me.

That thou hast her, it is not all my grief,
And yet it may be said I lov'd her dearly;
That she hath thee is of my wailing chief,
A loss in love that touches me more nearly.
Loving offenders, thus I will excuse ye:　　　5
Thou dost love her because thou know'st I love her,
And for my sake even so doth she abuse me,
Suff'ring my friend for my sake to approve her.
If I lose thee, my loss is my love's gain,
And losing her, my friend hath found that loss:　　10
Both find each other, and I lose both twain,
And both for my sake lay on me this cross.
　　But here's the joy — my friend and I are one.
　　Sweet flattery! then she loves but me alone.

SONNET 43. *1 wink* shut my eyes (in sleep). *2 unrespected* unnoticed and unworthy of notice. *4 darkly bright* (a) illuminated in the darkness (b) secretly cheerful. *are bright . . . directed* see clearly in the darkness (being themselves infused with the light of thee). *5 whose shadow . . . bright* whose image (shadow) illuminates the darkness (shadows). *6 thy shadow's form* the real form which your image represents. *form happy show* create a glorious display. *8 shade* shadow, image. *11 thy* CAPELL; Q: "their." *imperfect* without substance. *13 to see* (a) in appearance (b) in so far as ability to see is concerned. *14 show thee me* reveal you to me.

SONNET 44. This sonnet and the next one rest upon the notion that human life is composed of the four elements of earth, water, fire and air. Earth and water are the heavy elements, bound by gravity and dominant in the human body. Fire and air contain the human spirit and are light and free. *1 dull* heavy — i.e. earth and water. *2 Injurious* cruel and unjust. *4 limits* regions. *where* to where. *7 thought* i.e. air. *9 thought kills me* I am killed by the thought or knowledge. *11 so much . . . wrought* being so fully created of the heavy elements, earth and water. *12 attend . . . moan* wait weepingly until time is ready (to unite us). *13 naught* MALONE; Q: "naughts." *14 But heavy . . . woe* From the heavy elements the poet can receive only the "weight" and the "water" of his tears.

44

43

When most I wink, then do mine eyes best see,
For all the day they view things unrespected,
But when I sleep, in dreams they look on thee
And, darkly bright, are bright in dark directed.
Then thou, whose shadow shadows doth make bright,   5
How would thy shadow's form form happy show
To the clear day with thy much clearer light
When to unseeing eyes thy shade shines so!
How would, I say, mines eyes be blessed made
By looking on thee in the living day,   10
When in dead night thy fair imperfect shade
Through heavy sleep on sightless eyes doth stay!
 All days are nights to see till I see thee,
 And nights bright days when dreams do show thee me.

44

If the dull substance of my flesh were thought,
Injurious distance should not stop my way;
For then, despite of space, I would be brought,
From limits far remote, where thou dost stay.
No matter then although my foot did stand   5
Upon the farthest earth remov'd from thee;
For nimble thought can jump both sea and land
As soon as think the place where he would be.
But, ah, thought kills me that I am not thought,
To leap large lengths of miles when thou art gone, 10
But that, so much of earth and water wrought,
I must attend time's leisure with my moan,
 Receiving naught by elements so slow
 But heavy tears, badges of either's woe.

SONNET 45. *1 two* i.e. elements. *slight* insubstantial. *4 present-absent* now here, now there. *5 quicker* more lively. *7 four* four elements. *8 melancholy* supposedly caused by an excess of water and earth in the body. *9 life's composition* the proper balance of the four elements which make up life. *recured* restored to health. *10 swift messengers* i.e. letters, which the poet presumably has received from his friend. *11 even but now* at this very moment. *12 thy* MALONE; Q: "their."

SONNET 46. The sonnet supposes a legal contest between the poet's eye and his heart. The notion is a commonplace of Renaissance love poetry. *1 mortal* deadly. *2 conquest* (a) booty won in battle (b) goods awarded as the result of a lawsuit. *thy sight* the sight of you — your portrait. *3 Mine eye . . . would bar* my eye seeks to deny my heart the sight of your picture. *thy* CAPELL; Q: "their." Also in lines 8, 13 and 14. *4 freedom of* privilege of exercising. *6 closet* secret, locked up place. *with* by. *crystal* clear, penetrating. *9 'cide* decide (MALONE; Q: "side," which has been defended as meaning "settle" or "arrange"). *title* question of ownership. *10 quest* inquest, jury. *12 moiety* share (not necessarily a half).

46

❖❖❖❖❖❖❖❖❖ 45

The other two, slight air and purging fire,
Are both with thee, wherever I abide;
The first my thought, the other my desire,
These present-absent with swift motion slide.
For when these quicker elements are gone   5
In tender embassy of love to thee,
My life, being made of four, with two alone
Sinks down to death, oppress'd with melancholy;
Until life's composition be recured
By those swift messengers return'd from thee,   10
Who even but now come back again, assured
Of thy fair health, recounting it to me.
   This told, I joy; but then no longer glad,
    I send them back again and straight grow sad.

❖❖❖❖❖❖❖❖❖ 46

Mine eye and heart are at a mortal war
How to divide the conquest of thy sight;
Mine eye my heart thy picture's sight would bar,
My heart mine eye the freedom of that right.
My heart doth plead that thou in him dost lie   5
(A closet never pierc'd with crystal eyes);
But the defendant doth that plea deny
And says in him thy fair appearance lies.
To 'cide this title is impanneled
A quest of thoughts, all tenants to the heart,   10
And by their verdict is determined
The clear eye's moiety and the dear heart's part:
   As thus — mine eye's due is thy outward part,
    And my heart's right thy inward love of heart.

47

SONNET 47. *1 league is took* agreement is reached. *6 painted banquet* meal consisting of a painting. A "banquet" was literally a light desert of fruit and sweetmeats served after a main meal. *bids* invites. *10 Thyself away* although you yourself are away. *still* always. *art* CAPELL; Q: "are." *11 not* BENSON; Q: "nor."

SONNET 48. *1 took my way* left home to travel. *2 truest* most trustworthy. *4 hands of falsehood* thieves. *5 to whom* compared with whom. *6 worthy* precious. *7 only care* only thing I really value. *8 vulgar* common. *9 chest* (a) coffer (b) breast. *11 closure* enclosure. *12 part* go away. *14 truth* honesty.

48

Betwixt mine eye and heart a league is took,
And each doth good turns now unto the other.
When that mine eye is famish'd for a look,
Or heart in love with sighs himself doth smother,
With my love's picture then my eye doth feast   5
And to the painted banquet bids my heart.
Another time mine eye is my heart's guest
And in his thoughts of love doth share a part.
So, either by thy picture or my love,
Thyself away art present still with me;   10
For thou not farther than my thoughts canst move,
And I am still with them, and they with thee;
   Or, if they sleep, thy picture in my sight
    Awakes my heart to heart's and eye's delight.

How careful was I, when I took my way,
Each trifle under truest bars to thrust,
That to my use it might unused stay
From hands of falsehood, in sure wards of trust!
But thou, to whom my jewels trifles are,   5
Most worthy comfort, now my greatest grief,
Thou, best of dearest, and mine only care,
Art left the prey of every vulgar thief.
Thee have I not lock'd up in any chest,
Save where thou art not, though I feel thou art,   10
Within the gentle closure of my breast,
From whence at pleasure thou mayst come and part;
   And even thence thou wilt be stol'n, I fear,
    For truth proves thievish for a prize so dear.

SONNET 49. *1 Against* in anticipation of and preparation for. *2 defects* deficiencies. *3 Whenas* when. *cast . . . sum* reckoned up his final account. *4 advis'd respects* deliberate consideration (of all the elements) in our relationship. *5 strangely pass* go by me like a stranger. *7 converted* transformed. *8 of settled gravity* for a grave and sober attitude of coldness. *9 ensconce me* fortify myself. *10 desart* desert, merit. The Q spelling is retained to indicate the rhyme. *11–12 And this . . . thy part* and raise my hand, as a witness in a court of law, to testify against myself, in support of your rational argument for leaving me. The point is that the poet has no legal claim to his friend's affection, for love does not spring from rational or legal considerations. *14 to love* one should love. *cause* legal argument.

SONNET 50. *1 heavy* sadly. *3 that ease . . . repose* the accommodation and rest (which I seek at the end of my journey). *6 dully* MALONE; Q: "duly." *to bear* because he bears. *weight* sorrow. *8 being made from thee* i.e. since that speed is carrying me away from thee. *12 sharp* painful.

❖❖❖❖❖❖❖❖❖❖ 49

Against that time (if ever that time come)
When I shall see thee frown on my defects,
Whenas thy love hath cast his utmost sum,
Call'd to that audit by advis'd respects;
Against that time when thou shalt strangely pass   5
And scarcely greet me with that sun, thine eye,
When love, converted from the thing it was,
Shall reasons find of settled gravity —
Against that time do I ensconce me here
Within the knowledge of mine own desart,   10
And this my hand against myself uprear,
To guard the lawful reasons on thy part.
    To leave poor me thou hast the strength of laws,
    Since why to love I can allege no cause.

❖❖❖❖❖❖❖❖❖❖ 50

How heavy do I journey on the way
When what I seek (my weary travel's end)
Doth teach that ease and that repose to say,
"Thus far the miles are measur'd from thy friend!"
The beast that bears me, tired with my woe,   5
Plods dully on, to bear that weight in me,
As if by some instinct the wretch did know
His rider lov'd not speed, being made from thee.
The bloody spur cannot provoke him on
That sometimes anger thrusts into his hide;   10
Which heavily he answers with a groan,
More sharp to me than spurring to his side;
    For that same groan doth put this in my mind —
    My grief lies onward and my joy behind.

51

SONNET 51. *1 slow offence* offence of being slow. *4 of posting is no need* there is no need to ride at full speed. *6 swift extremity* extreme of swiftness. *8 In winged . . . I know* I would have no feeling of speed even though I were flying (so impatient would I be to reach you). *10–11 desire . . . fiery race* my desire to be with you, being made of the most perfect kind of love, like a horse, will neigh in the excitement of its fiery race to reach you, unlike the dull horse on which I am riding. *12–14 But love . . . to go* but I will thus excuse my horse who, out of love for me, walked slowly in taking me away from you. I will let him go on slowly, while I run to reach you before him. This seems to be the general meaning of these obscure and much debated lines. *jade* a horse of inferior quality. *go* walk.

SONNET 52. *1 So am I as* I am exactly like. *key* Pronounced to rhyme with "survey." *4 For blunting* so as not to blunt. *seldom pleasure* pleasure seldom experienced. *5 solemn* formal. *7 thinly placed* spread out. *8 captain* of superior worth. *carcanet* jewelled necklace. *12 new unfolding* freshly revealing. *his imprison'd pride* its hidden magnificence. *13–14 whose worthiness . . . to hope* whose excellence causes me to triumph when I see you and to hope for your sight when you are absent.

51

Thus can my love excuse the slow offence
Of my dull bearer when from thee I speed:
From where thou art, why should I haste me thence?
Till I return, of posting is no need.
O, what excuse will my poor beast then find   5
When swift extremity can seem but slow?
Then should I spur, though mounted on the wind,
In winged speed no motion shall I know.
Then can no horse with my desire keep pace;
Therefore desire, of perfect'st love being made,   10
Shall neigh (no dull flesh) in his fiery race;
But love, for love, thus shall excuse my jade:
   Since from thee going he went wilful slow,
   Towards thee I'll run and give him leave to go.

52

So am I as the rich whose blessed key
Can bring him to his sweet up-locked treasure,
The which he will not ev'ry hour survey,
For blunting the fine point of seldom pleasure.
Therefore are feasts so solemn and so rare,   5
Since, seldom coming, in the long year set,
Like stones of worth they thinly placed are,
Or captain jewels in the carcanet.
So is the time that keeps you as my chest,
Or as the wardrobe which the robe doth hide,   10
To make some special instant special blest
By new unfolding his imprison'd pride.
   Blessed are you, whose worthiness gives scope,
   Being had, to triumph, being lack'd, to hope.

SONNET 53. The sonnet reflects the platonic idea that all beautiful objects merely reflect the more perfect ideal forms of which they are emanations. Here the poet's friend is made to represent the ideal.   *2 strange shadows* images or reflections which are not a part of your own being. *tend* attend.   *3 shade* reflection, such as the single shadow which a man's body casts and which "tends" upon him.   *4 And you . . . shadow lend* and you, although you are but a single person, can supply an image for every other thing of beauty.   *5 counterfeit* description (of Adonis).   *8 tires* attires (such as Helen of Troy would wear).   *9 foison* harvest, autumn. *14 none you* no one is like you. *constant heart* That this seems hardly applicable to the friend whom the poet has been addressing has struck many commentators. Perhaps this sonnet is addressed to another person.

SONNET 54.   *2 By* because of. *truth* fidelity.   *3 deem* judge.   *5 canker blooms* blossoms of the canker-rose or wild dog-rose, which have only a very faint perfume.   *6 tincture* colour.   *7 wantonly* playfully.   *8 masked* concealed. *discloses* opens.   *9 for* because. *their virtue . . . show* their excellence consists only in appearance (and not in perfume as well).   *10 unrespected* unnoticed and neglected.   *11 Die to themselves* die without leaving any benefit to others (as the damask rose leaves its perfume after it has died).   *12 Of their . . . odours made* of their sweet-smelling remains perfumes are made.   *14 that* i.e. your beauty and youth. *vade* disappear, decay. *my verse* MALONE; Q, K: "by verse." *distills your truth* preserves the essence of your fidelity, as perfume preserves the essence of the rose.

54

53

What is your substance, whereof are you made,
That millions of strange shadows on you tend?
Since every one hath, every one, one shade,
And you, but one, can every shadow lend.
Describe Adonis, and the counterfeit   5
Is poorly imitated after you.
On Helen's cheek all art of beauty set,
And you in Grecian tires are painted new.
Speak of the spring, and foison of the year:
The one doth shadow of your beauty show,   10
The other as your bounty doth appear,
And you in every blessed shape we know.
   In all external grace you have some part,
    But you like none, none you, for constant heart.

54

O, how much more doth beauty beauteous seem
By that sweet ornament which truth doth give!
The rose looks fair, but fairer we it deem
For that sweet odour which doth in it live.
The canker blooms have full as deep a dye   5
As the perfumed tincture of the roses,
Hang on such thorns, and play as wantonly
When summer's breath their masked buds discloses;
But, for their virtue only is their show,
They live unwoo'd and unrespected fade,   10
Die to themselves. Sweet roses do not so:
Of their sweet deaths are sweetest odours made.
   And so of you, beauteous and lovely youth,
    When that shall vade, my verse distills your truth.

SONNET 55. The poet defies the ravages of time and affirms that through his verse the beauty of his friend will endure forever. The theme was a favourite one among Elizabethan sonneteers, having its roots in the classics, most notably in Horace (ODES, III,XXX,1–5) and Ovid (METAMORPHOSES, XV,871–9). *1 monuments* MALONE; Q: "monument." *2 rhyme* poem. *3 in these contents* in what these lines contain. *4 unswept stone* neglected monument (which would contain the dead man's epitaph, to which the poet is comparing his verse). *sluttish* dirty, untidy. *6 broils* battles, civil uprisings. *root out* uproot, destroy. *7 quick* lively, fierce. *9 'Gainst* in spite of. *all-oblivious enmity* oblivion which is the enemy of all mankind. *10 pace forth* go boldly and proudly on your way. *still* forever. *12 wear this world out* endure longer than this world. *ending doom* day of judgment. *13 judgment . . . arise* day of judgment when you yourself shall rise from the grave. *14 this* this poem. *in lovers' eyes* in the eyes of those who admire you.

SONNET 56. *1 love* the spirit of love (not the loved person). *2 edge* keenness. *appetite* lust. *3 but to-day* merely for the present moment (whereas love, unlike "appetite" is eternal). *4 his* its. *5 love* my friend. *6 wink* close in sleep. *8 dulness* insensibility. *9 sad int'rim* period of estrangement or separation. *10 contracted new* recently betrothed. *11 banks* seashore. *12 Return of love* the loved one's return. *13 Or call* MALONE; Q: "As call."

Not marble nor the gilded monuments
Of princes shall outlive this pow'rful rhyme;
But you shall shine more bright in these contents
Than unswept stone, besmear'd with sluttish time.
When wasteful war shall statues overturn,   5
And broils root out the work of masonry,
Nor Mars his sword nor war's quick fire shall burn
The living record of your memory.
'Gainst death and all-oblivious enmity
Shall you pace forth; your praise shall still find room   10
Even in the eyes of all posterity
That wear this world out to the ending doom.
    So, till the judgment that yourself arise,
      You live in this, and dwell in lovers' eyes.

Sweet love, renew thy force; be it not said
Thy edge should blunter be than appetite,
Which but to-day by feeding is allay'd,
To-morrow sharp'ned in his former might.
So, love, be thou: although to-day thou fill   5
Thy hungry eyes even till they wink with fulness,
To-morrow see again, and do not kill
The spirit of love with a perpetual dulness.
Let this sad int'rim like the ocean be
Which parts the shore where two contracted new   10
Come daily to the banks, that, when they see
Return of love, more blest may be the view;
    Or call it winter, which, being full of care,
      Makes summer's welcome thrice more wish'd, more
        rare.

SONNET 57. *1 tend* wait. *5 the world-without-end hour* the tedious hour which seems as though it will never end. *7 Nor think* nor do I dare to think. *8 servant* (a) attendant (b) lover. *9 question* dispute. *jealious* jealous, suspicious (an old form of the word). *10 your affairs suppose* speculate about what you are doing. *11 stay* wait. *12 Save . . . those* except how happy you are making those who are in your presence. *13 true* faithful. *will* desire, perversity. There may be a pun on the name "Will."

SONNET 58. *2 I should . . . control* that I should think of controlling. *3 th' account . . . crave* demand an accounting of how you have spent your time. *4 stay* wait for. *6 Th' imprison'd . . . liberty* the sense of imprisonment which I suffer because of your freedom to be absent from me. *7 tame to sufferance* subdued to endurance (as a horse is tamed to bear his rider). *bide each check* endure each rebuke. *8 injury* injustice, insult. *9 list* wish. *charter* acknowledged privilege (of rank). *10–11 privilege . . . you will* grant your time the privilege of being employed in whatever way you choose. *12 self-doing crime* crime committed by yourself. *13 I am to* I am obliged to.

57

Being your slave, what should I do but tend
Upon the hours and times of your desire?
I have no precious time at all to spend,
Nor services to do, till you require.
Nor dare I chide the world-without-end hour   5
Whilst I, my sovereign, watch the clock for you,
Nor think the bitterness of absence sour
When you have bid your servant once adieu.
Nor dare I question with my jealous thought
Where you may be, or your affairs suppose,   10
But, like a sad slave, stay and think of nought
Save where you are how happy you make those.
   So true a fool is love that in your will,
   Though you do anything, he thinks no ill.

58

That god forbid that made me first your slave
I should in thought control your times of pleasure,
Or at your hand th' account of hours to crave,
Being your vassal bound to stay your leisure!
O, let me suffer (being at your beck)   5
Th' imprison'd absence of your liberty;
And patience, tame to sufferance, bide each check
Without accusing you of injury.
Be where you list; your charter is so strong
That you yourself may privilege your time   10
To what you will; to you it doth belong
Yourself to pardon of self-doing crime.
   I am to wait, though waiting so be hell;
   Not blame your pleasure, be it ill or well.

59

SONNET 59. *1–2 If there be . . . been before* The cyclical theory of history, that everything which occurs in the present has occurred before, is a classical notion which Shakespeare may have encountered in various places. *that* everything. *2 beguil'd* cheated. *3 labouring for invention* searching for new subject matter. *3–4 bear amiss . . . former child* give birth mistakenly or improperly (miscarry) to a child which has already been born before. *5 record* memory. *6 courses of the sun* years. *7 antique* ancient. *8 mind . . . done* thoughts were expressed in writing. *10 To this . . . your frame* to your physical body, so wonderfully constructed. *11 Whether . . . they* whether we are improved (over men of that ancient time) or whether they were superior to us. *12 whether . . . same* whether the constant movement of time (historical cycles) leaves mankind unchanged. *13 wits* men of intellect.

SONNET 60. *4 sequent* successive. *forwards do contend* move steadily forward. *5 Nativity . . . light* the newborn child, once it moves into the sphere of light. *7 Crooked eclipses* malignant celestial influences. *8 confound* destroy. *9 transfix . . . youth* destroy the ornamentation with which youth is adorned. *10 delves the parallels* digs the creases. *11 rarities . . . truth* choicest features of nature's most perfect creation. *13 times in hope* future times. *14 his* Time's.

◇◇◇◇◇◇◇◇◇◇◇ 59

If there be nothing new, but that which is
Hath been before, how are our brains beguil'd,
Which, labouring for invention, bear amiss
The second burden of a former child!
O that record could with a backward look, 5
Even of five hundred courses of the sun,
Show me your image in some antique book,
Since mind at first in character was done!
That I might see what the old world could say
To this composed wonder of your frame; 10
Whether we are mended, or whe'r better they,
Or whether revolution be the same.
    O, sure I am the wits of former days
    To subjects worse have given admiring praise.

◇◇◇◇◇◇◇◇◇◇◇ 60

Like as the waves make towards the pebbled shore,
So do our minutes hasten to their end;
Each changing place with that which goes before,
In sequent toil all forwards do contend.
Nativity, once in the main of light, 5
Crawls to maturity, wherewith being crown'd,
Crooked eclipses 'gainst his glory fight,
And Time that gave doth now his gift confound.
Time doth transfix the flourish set on youth
And delves the parallels in beauty's brow, 10
Feeds on the rarities of nature's truth,
And nothing stands but for his scythe to mow;
    And yet to times in hope my verse shall stand,
    Praising thy worth, despite his cruel hand.

SONNET 61. *3 broken* A rare instance of assonance rather than full rhyme. *4 shadows* images (in dreams). *mock* deceive (by imitating your appearance). *7 To find . . . in me* to discover my faults and how badly I waste my time. *8 scope and tenure* extent and essential nature. *11 defeat* destroy. *13 watch* go without sleep. *wake* spend the night in revelling.

SONNET 62. *1 self-love* vanity, conceit. *5 gracious* handsome, pleasing. *6 true* perfect. *no truth . . . account* no perfection of such value and importance. *7-8 And for . . . worths surmount* and for my own satisfaction I consider my own merit as though it were greater than the merit of any other person. *9 glass* mirror. *myself indeed* what I truly am. *10 Beated* beaten. *chopt* chapped, creased, wrinkled. *antiquity* old age. *12 Self . . . iniquity* for such a person (as my mirror reveals) to love himself would be iniquity. *13 (myself)* who are myself. *14 Painting . . . thy days* adorning my old age with the beauty of your youth.

Is it thy will thy image should keep open
My heavy eyelids to the weary night?
Dost thou desire my slumbers should be broken
While shadows like to thee do mock my sight?
Is it thy spirit that thou send'st from thee   5
So far from home into my deeds to pry,
To find out shames and idle hours in me,
The scope and tenure of thy jealousy?
O, no! thy love, though much, is not so great.
It is my love that keeps mine eye awake;   10
Mine own true love that doth my rest defeat,
To play the watchman ever for thy sake.
    For thee watch I whilst thou dost wake elsewhere,
    From me far off, with others all too near.

Sin of self-love possesseth all mine eye
And all my soul and all my every part;
And for this sin there is no remedy,
It is so grounded inward in my heart.
Methinks no face so gracious is as mine,   5
No shape so true, no truth of such account,
And for myself mine own worth do define
As I all other in all worths surmount.
But when my glass shows me myself indeed,
Beated and chopt with tann'd antiquity,   10
Mine own self-love quite contrary I read;
Self so self-loving were iniquity.
    'Tis thee (myself) that for myself I praise,
    Painting my age with beauty of thy days.

SONNET 63. *1 Against* in anticipation of the time when. *2 injurious* destructive, insulting and unjust. *crush'd and o'erworn* crumpled and worn out (like old clothes). *5 travell'd* journeyed laboriously (Q: "trauaild"). "Travel" and "travail" were used interchangeably in Shakespeare's day. *age's steepy night* the precipitous plunge of old age into the darkness of death. *10 confounding* destroying. *knife* the proverbial scythe of Father Time. *12 though . . . life* although he take the life of my friend. *13 these black lines* the lines of the poem. *14 still* forever.

SONNET 64. *1 fell* cruel, fierce. *2 cost* expence (here specifically of buildings and monuments). *3 sometime* formerly. *rased* razed. *4 brass eternal* everlasting or impregnable brass. *slave . . . rage* controlled and subjugated by the fury of death. *6 Advantage* inroads. *8 Increasing . . . with store* The abundance (store) of the land grows less as the water eats it away and the abundance of the sea is thus increased. At the same time the abundance of land is increased and that of the sea decreased as the sea deposits sand upon the shore. *9 state* possessions. *10 state* worldly grandeur. *confounded to decay* wasted away to a condition of decay. *13 which* i.e. the thought. *14 to have* for having.

63

Against my love shall be as I am now,
With Time's injurious hand crush'd and o'erworn;
When hours have drain'd his blood, and fill'd his brow
With lines and wrinkles; when his youthful morn
Hath travell'd on to age's steepy night,   5
And all those beauties whereof now he's king
Are vanishing, or vanish'd out of sight,
Stealing away the treasure of his spring —
For such a time do I now fortify
Against confounding age's cruel knife,   10
That he shall never cut from memory
My sweet love's beauty, though my lover's life.
    His beauty shall in these black lines be seen,
    And they shall live, and he in them still green.

64

When I have seen by Time's fell hand defaced
The rich proud cost of outworn buried age;
When sometime lofty towers I see down rased,
And brass eternal slave to mortal rage;
When I have seen the hungry ocean gain   5
Advantage on the kingdom of the shore,
And the firm soil win of the wat'ry main,
Increasing store with loss, and loss with store;
When I have seen such interchange of state,
Or state itself confounded to decay;   10
Ruin hath taught me thus to ruminate,
That Time will come and take my love away.
    This thought is as a death, which cannot choose
    But weep to have that which it fears to lose.

SONNET 65. *1 Since* since there is neither. *2 sad mortality* calamitous destruction. *o'ersways their power* surpasses them in power. *4 action* vigour. *6 wrackful* destructive. *batt'ring days* The battering ram was a principal weapon used against cities under siege. *7 stout* sturdy. *8 decays* causes them to decay. *9–10 Where, alack . . . lie hid* where shall that jewel which Time most desires be hidden so that it can escape imprisonment in the chest where Time keeps all dead things he has garnered. *11 his* Time's. *12 spoil of* MALONE; Q: "spoil or." *forbid* prevent. *14 my love* my friend.

SONNET 66. *1 these* the following evils. *2 desert* the deserving man. *3 needy nothing* those in need of nothing. *trimm'd in jollity* dressed in festive clothing. *4 unhappily forsworn* miserably denounced on oath. *5 gilded honour* specious rank and position. *7 right* true, genuine. *disgrac'd* disparaged, denied proper reputation. *8 limping sway* feeble and ineffective government. *disabled* prevented from showing its ability. *9 art* all learning as well as the arts. *made . . . authority* rendered incapable of expression by censorship. *10 doctor-like* like a pedant. *11 simplicity* stupidity. *12 captain* dominant, controlling.

65

Since brass, nor stone, nor earth, nor boundless sea,
But sad mortality o'ersways their power,
How with this rage shall beauty hold a plea,
Whose action is no stronger than a flower?
O, how shall summer's honey breath hold out   5
Against the wrackful siege of batt'ring days,
When rocks impregnable are not so stout,
Nor gates of steel so strong, but Time decays?
O fearful meditation! Where, alack,
Shall Time's best jewel from Time's chest lie hid?   10
Or what strong hand can hold his swift foot back?
Or who his spoil of beauty can forbid?
   O, none! unless this miracle have might,
   That in black ink my love may still shine bright.

66

Tir'd with all these, for restful death I cry:
As, to behold desert a beggar born,
And needy nothing trimm'd in jollity,
And purest faith unhappily forsworn,
And gilded honour shamefully misplac'd,   5
And maiden virtue rudely strumpeted,
And right perfection wrongfully disgrac'd,
And strength by limping sway disabled,
And art made tongue-tied by authority,
And folly (doctor-like) controlling skill,   10
And simple truth miscall'd simplicity,
And captive good attending captain ill.
   Tir'd with all these, from these would I be gone,
   Save that, to die, I leave my love alone.

SONNET 67. *1 with infection* in an age of corruption (full of the evils listed in the previous sonnet). *2 grace* adorn, make beautiful. *4 lace* embellish. *5 false painting* the use of cosmetics (common among Elizabethan gallants). *6 dead seeing* lifeless appearance. Some editors read "seeming," a plausible emendation. *of* from. *7 poor* inferior. *indirectly* artificially, by imitation. *8 Roses of shadow* mere pictures of roses. *9–10 Why should . . . lively veins* why should he continue to live since bankrupt Nature is now so poorly supplied with blood that she cannot produce blushes by means of living veins (but must resort to cosmetics)? *11–12 For she . . . his gains* for Nature has no supply of beauty other than his, and, although she boasts of many beautiful persons, she subsists only upon his beauty. The implication of this obscure metaphor is that Nature uses his friend's beauty to adorn the other creatures of whom she is proud; what beauty they have is merely a copy of his. *13 stores* preserves. *14 these last so bad* these present evil days.

SONNET 68. *1 map* representation. *outworn* gone by. *2 as flowers do now* i.e. in their natural colours (unaided by cosmetics). *3 bastard . . . fair* illegitimate appearances of beauty. *born* Q: "borne," which is meaningful in the sense of "worn." The modern differentiation in the spelling of the two words was unknown in Shakespeare's day. *6 The right of sepulchres* which should rightfully belong in the grave. Wigs were made from hair taken from dead bodies. *9 holy antique hours* blessed former times. *11 green* foliage. *13 store* preserve. *14 Art* The antithesis of Art and Nature was conventional in Renaissance poetry.

67

Ah, wherefore with infection should he live
And with his presence grace impiety,
That sin by him advantage should achieve
And lace itself with his society?
Why should false painting imitate his cheek   5
And steal dead seeing of his living hue?
Why should poor beauty indirectly seek
Roses of shadow, since his rose is true?
Why should he live, now Nature bankrout is,
Beggar'd of blood to blush through lively veins?   10
For she hath no exchequer now but his,
And, proud of many, lives upon his gains.
   O, him she stores, to show what wealth she had
   In days long since, before these last so bad.

68

Thus is his cheek the map of days outworn,
When beauty liv'd and died as flowers do now,
Before these bastard signs of fair were born
Or durst inhabit on a living brow;
Before the golden tresses of the dead,   5
The right of sepulchres, were shorn away
To live a second life on second head;
Ere beauty's dead fleece made another gay.
In him those holy antique hours are seen,
Without all ornament, itself and true,   10
Making no summer of another's green,
Robbing no old to dress his beauty new;
   And him as for a map doth Nature store,
   To show false Art what beauty was of yore.

SONNET 69. *1-2 Those parts . . . can mend* your outward features as they are seen by the world are so perfect that the deepest thoughts of men cannot improve upon them. *3 due* CAPELL; Q: "end." *4 Utt'ring . . . commend* expressing no more than the bare truth (in the way that enemies would praise, giving no more than the absolute due). *5 Thy outward* your merely external (CAPELL; Q: "Their outward"). *outward praise* superficial praise by mere outsiders. *6 thine own* what is due you. *7 accents* words, expressions. *confound* destroy, contradict. *8 shown* seen. *10 in guess* as they interpret (thy deeds). *11 churls* misers (in their praise). *14 soil* (a) ground from which this springs (b) sully, blemish. *dost common grow* i.e. associate with base companions.

SONNET 70. *1 art* BENSON; Q: "are." *defect* fault. *2 mark* target. *was ever yet* has always been. *5 So thou be* provided that you are. *approve* prove. *6 Thy* CAPELL; Q: "Their." *being woo'd of time* since it (thy worth) is tempted by the evil persons of our age. *7 canker vice* vice which preys on beauty like a canker, a worm which feeds on rosebuds. *8 prime* youth. *9-10 Thou hast . . . being charg'd* That this is inconsistent with the sonnets which have gone before has bothered critics, but we cannot be sure of the order in which the poems were written. *charg'd* attacked. *11-12 Yet this . . . enlarg'd* yet the reputation you have earned cannot be so effective as to silence malice (envy) which is always rampant (enlarg'd). *13 suspect* suspicion. *mask'd not thy show* did not obscure your beautiful appearance. *14 Then thou . . . shouldst owe* then you would be unique, as a king who has the loyalty of every one of his subjects. *owe* own, possess.

69

Those parts of thee that the world's eye doth view
Want nothing that the thought of hearts can mend.
All tongues (the voice of souls) give thee that due,
Utt'ring bare truth, even so as foes commend.
Thy outward thus with outward praise is crown'd;   5
But those same tongues that give thee so thine own
In other accents do this praise confound
By seeing farther than the eye hath shown.
They look into the beauty of thy mind,
And that in guess they measure by thy deeds;   10
Then, churls, their thoughts (although their eyes were
    kind)
To thy fair flower add the rank smell of weeds;
    But why thy odour matcheth not thy show,
    The soil is this — that thou dost common grow.

70

That thou art blam'd shall not be thy defect,
For slander's mark was ever yet the fair;
The ornament of beauty is suspect,
A crow that flies in heaven's sweetest air.
So thou be good, slander doth but approve   5
Thy worth the greater, being woo'd of time;
For canker vice the sweetest buds doth love,
And thou present'st a pure unstained prime.
Thou hast pass'd by the ambush of young days,
Either not assail'd, or victor being charg'd;   10
Yet this thy praise cannot be so thy praise
To tie up envy, evermore enlarg'd.
    If some suspect of ill mask'd not thy show,
    Then thou alone kingdoms of hearts shouldst owe.

SONNET 71.   *8 on me* of me.   *make you woe* cause sorrow for you.   *10
compounded* blended, combined.   *11 rehearse* repeat.   *13 the wise world*
the knowing world, which will understand the shortcomings of the poet.
14 with me because of me.

SONNET 72.   *1 task you to recite* impose upon you the task of relating.
4 prove demonstrate.   *6 mine own desert* what I deserve.   *8 niggard*
stingy.   *11 My name be* let my name be.   *13 that . . . forth* my poetry.
Perhaps Shakespeare is discrediting his work for the public theatre, but
there is no way of knowing just what he is referring to, although there
has been ample speculation.   *14 should you* you would be.

◇◇◇◇◇◇◇◇◇◇ **71**

No longer mourn for me when I am dead
Than you shall hear the surly sullen bell
Give warning to the world that I am fled
From this vile world, with vilest worms to dwell.
Nay, if you read this line, remember not   5
The hand that writ it; for I love you so
That I in your sweet thoughts would be forgot
If thinking on me then should make you woe.
O, if, I say, you look upon this verse
When I, perhaps, compounded am with clay,   10
Do not so much as my poor name rehearse,
But let your love even with my life decay,
   Lest the wise world should look into your moan
   And mock you with me after I am gone.

◇◇◇◇◇◇◇◇◇◇ **72**

O, lest the world should task you to recite
What merit liv'd in me, that you should love
After my death, dear love, forget me quite,
For you in me can nothing worthy prove;
Unless you would devise some virtuous lie,   5
To do more for me than mine own desert
And hang more praise upon deceased I
Than niggard truth would willingly impart.
O, lest your true love may seem false in this,
That you for love speak well of me untrue,   10
My name be buried where my body is,
And live no more to shame nor me nor you!
   For I am sham'd by that which I bring forth,
   And so should you, to love things nothing worth.

SONNET 73. *3 against the cold* in anticipation of the threatening cold. *4 Bare ruin'd choirs* The limbs of the trees, barren of their leaves, are compared to the ruined abbeys with which the English countryside was dotted in Shakespeare's day (following their dissolution in 1535), and the birds of summer are compared to the choirboys who have departed. The "choir" was the part of the church in which services were sung. *ruin'd* BENSON; Q: "rn'wd." *late* recently. *7 by-and-by* presently. *8 Death's second self* sleep (conventionally conceived of in Renaissance poetry as a model or small imitation of death). *seals* closes. There may be a reference to the "seeling" or sewing up of the eyes of hawks. The words were indistinguishable in Shakespeare's day. *12 Consum'd . . . by* The dying fire, if not raked up, is smothered by the ashes of the very logs which had fed it when it was new. *14 leave* give up (not "depart from").

SONNET 74. *1 fell arrest* fatal arresting officer, death. *2 all* any. *bail* possibility of remission. *3 My life . . . interest* some part of my life is included in this line of verse. *4 still* forever. *stay* remain. *5 reviewest* rereadest. *6 consecrate* consecrated. *7 The earth . . . due* Cf. EC-CLESIASTES, XII,7: "Then shall the dust return to the earth as it was; and the spirit shall return unto God who gave it." *9 dregs* poor remainder, most worthless part. *11 a wretch's knife* the knife with which the Destiny, Atropos, cuts the thread of life. This is but one possible explanation. Others have seen the "knife" as the scythe wielded by Time. An allusion to the death of Christopher Marlowe, stabbed in a tavern in 1593, has sometimes been seen in the line. *12 of thee* by thee. *13–14 The worth . . . thee remains* the valuable part of the body is in the spirit which it contains, and that spirit is in my poetry, and that poetry remains with you.

✧✧✧✧✧✧✧✧✧ 73

That time of year thou mayst in me behold
When yellow leaves, or none, or few, do hang
Upon those boughs which shake against the cold,
Bare ruin'd choirs where late the sweet birds sang.
In me thou see'st the twilight of such day   5
As after sunset fadeth in the West,
Which by-and-by black night doth take away,
Death's second self, that seals up all in rest.
In me thou see'st the glowing of such fire
That on the ashes of his youth doth lie,   10
As the deathbed whereon it must expire,
Consum'd with that which it was nourish'd by.
   This thou perceiv'st, which makes thy love more
      strong,
   To love that well which thou must leave ere long.

✧✧✧✧✧✧✧✧✧ 74

But be contented. When that fell arrest
Without all bail shall carry me away,
My life hath in this line some interest,
Which for memorial still with thee shall stay.
When thou reviewest this, thou dost review   5
The very part was consecrate to thee.
The earth can have but earth, which is his due;
My spirit is thine, the better part of me.
So then thou hast but lost the dregs of life,
The prey of worms, my body being dead —   10
The coward conquest of a wretch's knife,
Too base of thee to be remembered.
   The worth of that is that which it contains,
   And that is this, and this with thee remains.

SONNET 75. *2 sweet-season'd* (a) coming in the sweet season of April (b) imbued with sweetness. *3 peace of you* peace I experience when I am with you. *hold* endure. *5 enjoyer* possessor. *6 Doubting* fearing that. *8 better'd* made happier. *11–12 Possessing . . . be took* possessing no delight but what is had from you, pursuing no delight but what must be taken from you. *13 pine* starve. *surfeit* overeat. *14 Or gluttoning* either overeating. *or all away* or having nothing to eat at all.

SONNET 76. *1 pride* ornamentation, elaboration. Shakespeare may be referring to the rhetoric of the metaphysical poets. *2 variation* variety. *quick* lively. *change* shifting conceits. *3 with the time* following the current fashion. *glance* turn. *4 compounds* compound words, neologisms. *5 still all one* always in the same manner. *6 keep . . . weed* keep on writing in my well-known poetic style — in the same old dress (weed). *7 tell* CAPELL; Q: "fel." *8 where* from whom. *10 argument* subject matter. *11–12 So all . . . already spent* thus the best of which I am capable is the fresh rearrangement of old words, using again the terms I have already used before. *14 still* forever. *is told* has been told.

76

So are you to my thoughts as food to life,
Or as sweet-season'd showers are to the ground;
And for the peace of you I hold such strife
As 'twixt a miser and his wealth is found:
Now proud as an enjoyer, and anon   5
Doubting the filching age will steal his treasure;
Now counting best to be with you alone,
Then better'd that the world may see my pleasure;
Sometime all full with feasting on your sight,
And by-and-by clean starved for a look;   10
Possessing or pursuing no delight
Save what is had or must from you be took.
   Thus do I pine and surfeit day by day,
   Or gluttoning on all, or all away.

Why is my verse so barren of new pride?
So far from variation or quick change?
Why, with the time, do I not glance aside
To new-found methods and to compounds strange?
Why write I still all one, ever the same,   5
And keep invention in a noted weed,
That every word doth almost tell my name,
Showing their birth, and where they did proceed?
O, know, sweet love, I always write of you,
And you and love are still my argument: 10
So all my best is dressing old words new,
Spending again what is already spent;
   For as the sun is daily new and old,
   So is my love still telling what is told.

SONNET 77. The sonnet was written to accompany the gift of a note-book, a mirror and a pocket sundial. *1 glass* mirror. *wear* are worn away (Q: "were"). *2 dial* sundial. *3 vacant leaves* blank pages. *thy mind's imprint* i.e. the thoughts you will write down. *4 this learning . . . taste* may you come to experience this knowledge (that the mirror and the sundial tell you). *6 mouthed* gaping, ready to devour. *give thee memory* remind you. *7 shady stealth* slowly moving shadow. *9 Look what* whatever (a common Elizabethan idiom). *10 waste* empty. *blanks* pages (THEOBALD; Q: "blacks"). *10–12 thou shalt . . . thy mind* you will see those children of your brain taken care of and protected, so that when you reread them later they will convey new meaning, like children who have grown up. *13 offices* duties (of committing your thoughts to the pages and later rereading them).

SONNET 78. *2 fair assistance* (a) favourable inspiration (b) benevolent patronage. Either or both meanings may have been intended. *3 alien* belonging to outsiders. *got my use* followed my practice (of writing poems to you). *4 under thee* (a) in your service (b) enjoying your patronage. *disperse* disseminate, publish. *5 on high* aloud. *7 the learned's wing* This would suggest that the "rival poet" was a learned man. The meta-phor is from falconry. Broken feathers were replaced by a kind of grafting or "imping." *8 grace* excellence, beauty. There may be a pun on "grace" in the sense of a university degree, indicating that the "rival poet" was a university man. *10 influence* inspiration. The word is an astrological term indicating specifically the power exerted by a star. *12 And arts . . . graced be* and learning by your beauty and excellence is embellished. *13 advance* raise up.

77

Thy glass will show thee how thy beauties wear,
Thy dial how thy precious minutes waste.
The vacant leaves thy mind's imprint will bear,
And of this book this learning mayst thou taste.
The wrinkles which thy glass will truly show,   5
Of mouthed graves will give thee memory.
Thou by thy dial's shady stealth mayst know
Time's thievish progress to eternity.
Look what thy memory cannot contain,
Commit to these waste blanks, and thou shalt find   10
Those children nurs'd, deliver'd from thy brain,
To take a new acquaintance of thy mind.
   These offices, so oft as thou wilt look,
   Shall profit thee and much enrich thy book.

78

So oft have I invok'd thee for my Muse
And found such fair assistance in my verse
As every alien pen hath got my use
And under thee their poesy disperse.
Thine eyes, that taught the dumb on high to sing   5
And heavy ignorance aloft to fly,
Have added feathers to the learned's wing
And given grace a double majesty.
Yet be most proud of that which I compile,
Whose influence is thine, and born of thee.   10
In others' works thou dost but mend the style,
And arts with thy sweet graces graced be;
   But thou art all my art and dost advance
   As high as learning my rude ignorance.

SONNET 79. *1 I alone* only I (and no other poet or poets). *2 had . . . grace* (a) received all of your favour (b) was full of your refined beauty. *3 gracious numbers* pleasing verses. *are decay'd* have fallen from favour. *4 give another place* yield my place to another poet. *5 thy lovely argument* the theme of your loveliness. *6 travail* labour. *7 what of thee* whatever qualities of yours. *thy poet* (a) any poet who writes of you (b) the "rival poet" in particular. Either meaning is possible. *invent* compose. *11 afford* offer. *14 owes thee* The poem is regarded as a debt owed by the poet to his patron.

SONNET 80. *1 faint* am discouraged. *2 a better spirit* a more gifted poet. *3 spends all his might* employs all his powers. *4 speaking* when I try to speak. *6 humble* humblest. *as* as well as. *7 saucy* impudent, daring. *8 wilfully* recklessly. *9 shallowest* most insignificant. *10 soundless* deepest, unfathomed. *11 wrack'd* shipwrecked. *12 of tall building* of large and stout construction (a nautical term). *goodly pride* great splendour. *14 my decay* the cause of my destruction.

Whilst I alone did call upon thy aid,
My verse alone had all thy gentle grace;
But now my gracious numbers are decay'd,
And my sick Muse doth give another place.
I grant, sweet love, thy lovely argument   5
Deserves the travail of a worthier pen;
Yet what of thee thy poet doth invent
He robs thee of, and pays it thee again.
He lends thee virtue, and he stole that word
From thy behaviour. Beauty doth he give,   10
And found it in thy cheek. He can afford
No praise to thee but what in thee doth live.
    Then thank him not for that which he doth say,
    Since what he owes thee thou thyself dost pay.

O, how I faint when I of you do write,
Knowing a better spirit doth use your name
And in the praise thereof spends all his might
To make me tongue-tied, speaking of your fame!
But since your worth, wide as the ocean is,   5
The humble as the proudest sail doth bear,
My saucy bark, inferior far to his,
On your broad main doth wilfully appear.
Your shallowest help will hold me up afloat
Whilst he upon your soundless deep doth ride;   10
Or, being wrack'd, I am a worthless boat,
He of tall building and of goodly pride.
    Then if he thrive, and I be cast away,
    The worst was this: my love was my decay.

SONNET 81. *1 Or* either. *3 From hence* from the earth. *4 in me each part* every one of my qualities. *5 from hence* from these poems. *6 to all the world* in so far as all men are concerned. *7 but a common grave* merely an ordinary undistinguished grave. *8 entombed in men's eyes* memorialized (as in a monumental tomb) in the eyes of the men who read my poems. *11 rehearse* recite. *13 virtue* power. *14 breath most breathes* language is most alive.

SONNET 82. *2 attaint* dishonour. *o'erlook* read over. *3 dedicated words* (a) words in a dedication of a book to a patron (b) words consecrated to their subject. *4 blessing every book* causing every book they write to be blessed (in being read by the friend). *5 hue* complexion, beauty. *6 Finding* The subject is "Thou." *limit* extent, reach. The unlearned poet is incapable of praising his friend's "knowledge" as his more learned "rival poet" apparently has done. *8 Some fresher . . . days* some newer representation of yourself (stamp) written in the manner of these superior days (in which poetic techniques have so improved). *10 What* whatever. *strained* exaggerated. *11–12 Thou, truly . . . true-telling friend* you, being truly beautiful, would be most truthfully represented in the simple words of your friend who speaks the truth (rather than in the rhetorical exaggerations of other poets). *14 in thee* in applying it to thee.

82

✧✧✧✧✧✧✧✧✧ 81

Or I shall live your epitaph to make,
Or you survive when I in earth am rotten.
From hence your memory death cannot take,
Although in me each part will be forgotten.
Your name from hence immortal life shall have,   5
Though I, once gone, to all the world must die.
The earth can yield me but a common grave
When you entombed in men's eyes shall lie.
Your monument shall be my gentle verse,
Which eyes not yet created shall o'erread;   10
And tongues to be your being shall rehearse
When all the breathers of this world are dead.
 You still shall live (such virtue hath my pen)
 Where breath most breathes, even in the mouths of
  men.

✧✧✧✧✧✧✧✧✧ 82

I grant thou wert not married to my Muse
And therefore mayst without attaint o'erlook
The dedicated words which writers use
Of their fair subject, blessing every book.
Thou art as fair in knowledge as in hue,   5
Finding thy worth a limit past my praise;
And therefore art enforc'd to seek anew
Some fresher stamp of the time-bettering days.
And do so, love; yet when they have devis'd
What strained touches rhetoric can lend,   10
Thou, truly fair, wert truly sympathiz'd
In true plain words by thy true-telling friend;
 And their gross painting might be better us'd
 Where cheeks need blood; in thee it is abus'd.

SONNET 83. *1 painting* artificial beautifying.   *2 fair* beauty. *set* applied.
4 The barren . . . debt the fruitless offering with which a poet attempts
to repay his patron.   *5 slept in your report* neglected to flatter you.   *6
being extant* simply being alive.   *7 modern quill* ordinary, commonplace
pen.   *8 Speaking of worth* when it writes of true value. *what worth* of
what worth. *grow* exist.   *9 silence* failure to flatter you.   *11 impair*
harm.   *12 bring a tomb* create only an elaborate lifeless monument.

SONNET 84. *3–4 In whose . . . equal grew* in what poet's treasury is
stored up such beauty as would be necessary to depict your equal. The
poet's treasury is conceived of as a walled-in (immured) garden where
beauty grows.   *7–8 can tell . . . are you* can describe you exactly as you
are. *so* in that way.   *10 clear* glorious.   *11 counterpart* copy, representation. *fame his wit* make him famous for his poetic skill.   *13 your
beauteous blessings* the beauty with which you are blessed.   *14 fond on*
foolishly addicted to. *makes . . . worse* (a) detracts from your worth (b)
makes all praise inadequate.

84

I never saw that you did painting need,
And therefore to your fair no painting set;
I found (or thought I found) you did exceed
The barren tender of a poet's debt;
And therefore have I slept in your report, 5
That you yourself, being extant, well might show
How far a modern quill doth come too short,
Speaking of worth, what worth in you doth grow.
This silence for my sin you did impute,
Which shall be most my glory, being dumb; 10
For I impair not beauty, being mute,
When others would give life, and bring a tomb.
   There lives more life in one of your fair eyes
   Than both your poets can in praise devise.

Who is it that says most which can say more
Than this rich praise — that you alone are you?
In whose confine immured is the store
Which should example where your equal grew.
Lean penury within that pen doth dwell 5
That to his subject lends not some small glory;
But he that writes of you, if he can tell
That you are you, so dignifies his story.
Let him but copy what in you is writ,
Not making worse what nature made so clear, 10
And such a counterpart shall fame his wit,
Making his style admired everywhere.
   You to your beauteous blessings add a curse,
   Being fond on praise, which makes your praises worse.

SONNET 85. *1 in manners . . . still* politely remains silent. *2 comments of your praise* treatises in praise of you. *compil'd* composed. *3 Reserve . . . quill* preserve what they have written with golden pen. This is a likely meaning, but the line has been much debated and may well be textually corrupt. *4 fil'd* polished, refined. *6 still* always. *7 able spirit* more talented poet. *affords* offers. *10 most* utmost. *13 Then . . . respect* then pay attention to others for the words they speak. *14 Me for . . . effect* to me for my unspoken thoughts, which speak in action (rather than in words).

SONNET 86. *1 proud* (a) stately, splendid (b) self-confident. The line has been used by some scholars to identify the "rival poet" with Marlowe, by others with Chapman. *3 ripe* mature, ready to be expressed. *inhearse* bury as in a coffin. *5 by spirits . . . write* The line has been applied to Marlowe, author of DOCTOR FAUSTUS, and to Chapman, whose interests in the occult were well known. *6 pitch* height. In falconry, the highest point to which a falcon may soar. *7 compeers by night* Either (a) books which he studies at night (b) supernatural spirits who visit him at night, or (c) friends with whom he engages in necromantic activities at night. *8 astonished* amazed, struck dumb. The word is much stronger than in modern usage. *9 that . . . ghost* The allusion appears to be some spirit, either alive or in books, who assists the "rival poet." There have been endless conjectures. *10 gulls . . . intelligence* deludes him with secret or mysterious information. Again the specific allusion is obscure. *12 from thence* from that quarter. *13 countenance* (a) support, patronage (b) appearance, physical beauty. *fill'd up* supplied what was lacking in. *14 mine* my verse.

85

My tongue-tied Muse in manners holds her still
While comments of your praise, richly compil'd,
Reserve their character with golden quill
And precious phrase by all the Muses fil'd.
I think good thoughts whilst other write good words,   5
And, like unlettered clerk, still cry "Amen"
To every hymn that able spirit affords
In polish'd form of well-refined pen.
Hearing you prais'd, I say " 'Tis so, 'tis true!"
And to the most of praise add something more;   10
But that is in my thought, whose love to you,
Though words come hindmost, holds his rank before.
　　Then others for the breath of words respect;
　　Me for my dumb thoughts, speaking in effect.

86

Was it the proud full sail of his great verse,
Bound for the prize of all-too-precious you,
That did my ripe thoughts in my brain inhearse,
Making their tomb the womb wherein they grew?
Was it his spirit, by spirits taught to write   5
Above a mortal pitch, that struck me dead?
No, neither he, nor his compeers by night
Giving him aid, my verse astonished.
He, nor that affable familiar ghost
Which nightly gulls him with intelligence,   10
As victors, of my silence cannot boast —
I was not sick of any fear from thence;
　　But when your countenance fill'd up his line,
　　Then lack'd I matter; that enfeebled mine.

SONNET 87. *1 dear* (a) precious, costly (b) of high rank. *2 estimate* value. *3 charter of thy worth* privilege of your rank. *releasing* freedom from all obligations. *4 determinate* ended (because his friend's "charter" releases him from obligation to honour the "bonds" of friendship. The term is a legal one). *5 hold* possess. *6 riches* The word was often used as a singular. *7–8 The cause . . . is swerving* since I have given you nothing in return for this fair gift (of your friendship) my title to it reverts to you. *11 upon misprision growing* having originated in an error of judgment. *12 on . . . making* on your making a better judgment. *14 a king* i.e. the poet. *no such matter* nothing of the kind.

SONNET 88. *1 set me light* place little value on me, despise me. *2 place . . . scorn* look scornfully upon what merit I have. *4 art forsworn* have broken your vow. *6 Upon thy part* in support of your case (against me). *7 conceal'd* secret. *attainted* tainted, infected. *8 That* so that. *shalt* K; Q: "shall." *10 bending* directing. *12 Doing thee . . . vantage me* in doing good to you do double good to myself (since I will have your good as well as my own). *14 right* advantage.

87

Farewell! thou art too dear for my possessing,
And like enough thou know'st thy estimate.
The charter of thy worth gives thee releasing;
My bonds in thee are all determinate.
For how do I hold thee but by thy granting,   5
And for that riches where is my deserving?
The cause of this fair gift in me is wanting,
And so my patent back again is swerving.
Thyself thou gav'st, thy own worth then not knowing,
Or me, to whom thou gav'st it, else mistaking: 10
So thy great gift, upon misprision growing,
Comes home again, on better judgment making.
   Thus have I had thee as a dream doth flatter —
   In sleep a king, but waking no such matter.

88

When thou shalt be dispos'd to set me light
And place my merit in the eye of scorn,
Upon thy side against myself I'll fight
And prove thee virtuous, though thou art forsworn.
With mine own weakness being best acquainted,   5
Upon thy part I can set down a story
Of faults conceal'd wherein I am attainted,
That thou, in losing me, shalt win much glory.
And I by this will be a gainer too;
For, bending all my loving thoughts on thee,   10
The injuries that to myself I do,
Doing thee vantage, double vantage me.
   Such is my love, to thee I so belong,
   That for thy right myself will bear all wrong.

SONNET 89. *1 Say* suppose. *2 comment* enlarge, expatiate. *3 straight* immediately. *halt* limp. *4 reasons* arguments. *5 disgrace* discredit, dishonour, remove from grace. *6 To set . . . change* to give an appropriate shape to whatever alteration you desire. *8 I will . . . strange* I will put an end to our familiarity and look upon you as though we did not know one another. *9 Be absent . . . walks* avoid the places where you walk. *11 profane* unworthy of your sacred presence. *12 haply* by chance. *13 debate* a quarrel.

SONNET 90. *2 my deeds* whatever I do. *cross* thwart, frustrate. *4 drop . . . after-loss* unexpectedly visit me to bring a future sorrow. *6 in the rearward . . . woe* following immediately after a sorrow which I have already conquered by learning to accept it. The image is that of waves of soldiers following closely upon one another. *8 linger out* protract, draw out. *purpos'd* intended. *10 petty griefs* lesser sorrows. *11 onset* first wave of attack (as opposed to "rearward"). *taste* experience. *13 strains* (a) kinds (b) stresses, feelings.

89

Say that thou didst forsake me for some fault,
And I will comment upon that offence.
Speak of my lameness, and I straight will halt,
Against thy reasons making no defence.
Thou canst not, love, disgrace me half so ill,   5
To set a form upon desired change,
As I'll myself disgrace, knowing thy will.
I will acquaintance strangle and look strange,
Be absent from thy walks, and in my tongue
Thy sweet beloved name no more shall dwell,   10
Lest I (too much profane) should do it wrong
And haply of our old acquaintance tell.
    For thee, against myself I'll vow debate,
    For I must ne'er love him whom thou dost hate.

90

Then hate me when thou wilt! if ever, now!
Now, while the world is bent my deeds to cross,
Join with the spite of fortune, make me bow,
And do not drop in for an after-loss.
Ah, do not, when my heart hath scap'd this sorrow,   5
Come in the rearward of a conquer'd woe;
Give not a windy night a rainy morrow,
To linger out a purpos'd overthrow.
If thou wilt leave me, do not leave me last,
When other petty griefs have done their spite,   10
But in the onset come. So shall I taste
At first the very worst of fortune's might;
    And other strains of woe, which now seem woe,
    Compar'd with loss of thee will not seem so.

91

SONNET 91. *1 birth* noble birth. *skill* art, knowledge and intelligence. The word was much broader in meaning than it is today. *2 force* strength. *3 newfangled ill* ugly in the latest fashion. *5 humour* disposition, individual temperament. *his* its. *adjunct* corresponding. *7 But these . . . measure* but none of these particular sources of pleasure is equal to the kind of pleasure I enjoy. *8 All these . . . general best* I improve upon all of these pleasures by having one pleasure which includes them all. *9 better* MALONE; Q: "bitter." *12 of all men's pride* of everything that other men take pride in possessing.

SONNET 92. *2 term of life* my (the poet's) lifetime. A legal expression. *5–6 Then need . . . hath end* then I need not fear the greatest of evils (complete alienation from you) for I will be killed by the slightest evil (the first sign of coldness from you). *8 humour* whim, caprice. *9–10 Thou canst . . . doth lie* you cannot continue to hurt me with infidelity since your first turning away from me will kill me. *11 happy title* title to happiness. *12 happy to die* because in my death I will escape the sorrow of losing your friendship. *14 I know it not* i.e. and thus, being deceived, I would be denied the fortunate death which would otherwise enable me to escape the pain of total loss of your friendship.

91

Some glory in their birth, some in their skill,
Some in their wealth, some in their body's force;
Some in their garments, though newfangled ill;
Some in their hawks and hounds, some in their horse;
And every humour hath his adjunct pleasure,   5
Wherein it finds a joy above the rest;
But these particulars are not my measure:
All these I better in one general best.
Thy love is better than high birth to me,
Richer than wealth, prouder than garments' cost,   10
Of more delight than hawks or horses be,
And having thee, of all men's pride I boast —
    Wretched in this alone, that thou mayst take
    All this away and me most wretched make.

92

But do thy worst to steal thyself away,
For term of life thou art assured mine;
And life no longer than thy love will stay,
For it depends upon that love of thine.
Then need I not to fear the worst of wrongs   5
When in the least of them my life hath end.
I see a better state to me belongs
Than that which on thy humour doth depend.
Thou canst not vex me with inconstant mind,
Since that my life on thy revolt doth lie.   10
O, what a happy title do I find,
Happy to have thy love, happy to die!
    But what's so blessed-fair that fears no blot?
    Thou mayst be false, and yet I know it not.

SONNET 93. *1 So* in that way (as suggested in the last line of the previous sonnet). *2 face* appearance. *3 seem* falsely express. *8 moods* external signs of angry disposition. *strange* unusual. *9 in thy creation* when you were created. *13 Eve's apple* i.e. beautiful on the outside, but corrupt and dangerous within. *grow* become. *14 answer not thy show* fail to accord with your external appearance.

SONNET 94. *1 will do none* do not desire to do injury. *2 do show* seem to do. *5–6 They rightly . . . from expense* they use the gifts of heaven as they should be used and carefully guard the riches of nature from waste. *7 lords . . . faces* permanent owners of whatever qualities are visible in their appearances. *8 stewards* temporary caretakers of beauty who dispense it for the advantage of others. *10 to itself* for its own benefit. *12 outbraves* makes a more magnificent show than. *his* its. *13 by their deeds* by acting in an evil way. *14 fester* rot.

93

So shall I live, supposing thou art true,
Like a deceived husband; so love's face
May still seem love to me, though alter'd new —
Thy looks with me, thy heart in other place.
For there can live no hatred in thine eye;   5
Therefore in that I cannot know thy change.
In many's looks the false heart's history
Is writ in moods and frowns and wrinkles strange;
But heaven in thy creation did decree
That in thy face sweet love should ever dwell;   10
Whate'er thy thoughts or thy heart's workings be,
Thy looks should nothing thence but sweetness tell.
 How like Eve's apple doth thy beauty grow
 If thy sweet virtue answer not thy show!

94

They that have pow'r to hurt and will do none,
That do not do the thing they most do show,
Who, moving others, are themselves as stone,
Unmoved, cold, and to temptation slow —
They rightly do inherit heaven's graces   5
And husband nature's riches from expense;
They are the lords and owners of their faces,
Others but stewards of their excellence.
The summer's flow'r is to the summer sweet,
Though to itself it only live and die;   10
But if that flow'r with base infection meet,
The basest weed outbraves his dignity:
 For sweetest things turn sourest by their deeds;
 Lilies that fester smell far worse than weeds.

95

SONNET 95. *1 lovely* lovable. *2 canker* caterpillar which feeds on rosebuds. *3 budding name* developing reputation. *5 thy days* how you spend your days. *6 sport* amorous adventures. *8 Naming . . . report* the mere mention of your name removes the stigma from any evil deeds that are reported of you. *9 mansion* magnificent dwelling place. *13 large privilege* unlimited sexual freedom. *14 hardest* sharpest.

SONNET 96. *1 wantonness* lechery. *2 gentle* aristocratic, high-minded. *sport* amorous adventures. *3 of more and less* by people of high rank and of low. *4 Thou mak'st . . . resort* you make graces out of the faults which reside in you. *8 translated* transformed. *deem'd* judged to be. *9 stern* cruel. *10 If like . . . translate* if he could transform his appearance into that of a lamb. *11 away* astray. *12 strength . . . state* full extent of your power. *13–14 But do . . . good report* This same couplet is used to end Sonnet 36. *mine . . . report* your good reputation is in my keeping.

◇◇◇◇◇◇◇◇◇◇ 95

How sweet and lovely dost thou make the shame
Which, like a canker in the fragrant rose,
Doth spot the beauty of thy budding name!
O, in what sweets dost thou thy sins enclose!
That tongue that tells the story of thy days   5
(Making lascivious comments on thy sport)
Cannot dispraise but in a kind of praise:
Naming thy name blesses an ill report.
O, what a mansion have those vices got
Which for their habitation chose out thee,   10
Where beauty's veil doth cover every blot
And all things turns to fair that eyes can see!
    Take heed, dear heart, of this large privilege.
    The hardest knife ill us'd doth lose his edge.

◇◇◇◇◇◇◇◇◇◇ 96

Some say thy fault is youth, some wantonness;
Some say thy grace is youth and gentle sport.
Both grace and faults are lov'd of more and less;
Thou mak'st faults graces that to thee resort.
As on the finger of a throned queen   5
The basest jewel will be well esteem'd,
So are those errors that in thee are seen
To truths translated and for true things deem'd.
How many lambs might the stern wolf betray
If like a lamb he could his looks translate!   10
How many gazers mightst thou lead away
If thou wouldst use the strength of all thy state!
    But do not so. I love thee in such sort
    As, thou being mine, mine is thy good report.

SONNET 97. *2 pleasure* most pleasing part. *5 time remov'd* period of my separation from you. *6 teeming* fertile, prolific. *big* pregnant. *increase* harvest (conceived of as the child of autumn). *7 Bearing . . . prime* giving birth to the fruit of the spring's amorousness. *9 abundant issue* rich progeny. *10 hope . . . fruit* unborn children and uncreated fruit. *11 wait on thee* are your servants to command. *13 cheer* cheerfulness.

SONNET 98. *2 proud-pied* splendidly variegated. *trim* ornamentation (literally, "clothes"). *4 heavy* sober, sad. *Saturn* the planet believed to cause melancholy in men. *5 Yet nor* yet neither. *lays* songs. *6 different flowers in* flowers differing in. *7 summer's story tell* write in a happy manner. *8 proud* showy. *9 wonder at* admire. *11 but figures* mere representations. *14 As with . . . play* I played with these flowers as I might play with a mere picture of you.

98

❖❖❖❖❖❖❖❖❖❖ 97

How like a winter hath my absence been
From thee, the pleasure of the fleeting year!
What freezings have I felt, what dark days seen!
What old December's bareness everywhere!
And yet this time remov'd was summer's time,   5
The teeming autumn, big with rich increase,
Bearing the wanton burden of the prime,
Like widowed wombs after their lords' decease;
Yet this abundant issue seem'd to me
But hope of orphans and unfathered fruit;   10
For summer and his pleasures wait on thee,
And, thou away, the very birds are mute;
   Or, if they sing, 'tis with so dull a cheer
   That leaves look pale, dreading the winter's near.

❖❖❖❖❖❖❖❖❖❖ 98

From you have I been absent in the spring,
When proud-pied April, dress'd in all his trim,
Hath put a spirit of youth in everything,
That heavy Saturn laugh'd and leapt with him,
Yet nor the lays of birds, nor the sweet smell   5
Of different flowers in odour and in hue,
Could make me any summer's story tell,
Or from their proud lap pluck them where they grew;
Nor did I wonder at the lily's white,
Nor praise the deep vermilion in the rose: 10
They were but sweet, but figures of delight,
Drawn after you, you pattern of all those.
   Yet seem'd it winter still, and, you away,
   As with your shadow I with these did play.

SONNET 99. An unusual fifteen-line sonnet.   *1 forward* early, spring-time. *chide* rebuke.   *3 pride* splendour.   *5 grossly* obviously.   *6 for thy hand* for attempting to imitate the whiteness of your hand.   *7 thy hair* He may mean the perfume rather than the colour of his friend's hair. The comparison of hair to marjoram buds has occasioned much comment.   *8 fearfully* conscious of their guilt.   *9 One* MALONE; Q: "Our." *13 eat* ate.   *15 sweet* sweet smell. Some editors would read "scent."

SONNET 100. *1–2 Where art . . . thy might* The poet addresses his Muse upon resuming sonnet writing after a lapse of some time, devoted probably to writing for the stage.   *3 fury* poetic inspiration (conceived of conventionally as a kind of frenzy). *worthless* ignoble.   *4 Dark'ning* diminishing. *lend* give. *base* inferior.   *5 straight* at once. *6 gentle numbers* noble verse. *idly* (a) foolishly (b) uselessly.   *7 lays* songs.   *8 argument* subject matter.   *9 resty* indolent.   *10 If* to see whether.   *11 be a satire to decay* write satires on the ruins of time (a conventional subject of the day).   *14 So thou prevent'st* in that way you will forestall.

100

The forward violet thus did I chide:
Sweet thief, whence didst thou steal thy sweet that
    smells,
If not from my love's breath? The purple pride
Which on thy soft cheek for complexion dwells
In my love's veins thou hast too grossly dy'd.   5
The lily I condemned for thy hand;
And buds of marjoram had stol'n thy hair.
The roses fearfully on thorns did stand,
One blushing shame, another white despair;
A third, nor red nor white, had stol'n of both,   10
And to his robb'ry had annex'd thy breath;
But, for his theft, in pride of all his growth
A vengeful canker eat him up to death.
    More flowers I noted, yet I none could see
    But sweet or colour it had stol'n from thee.   15

Where art thou, Muse, that thou forget'st so long
To speak of that which gives thee all thy might?
Spend'st thou thy fury on some worthless song,
Dark'ning thy pow'r to lend base subjects light?
Return, forgetful Muse, and straight redeem   5
In gentle numbers time so idly spent.
Sing to the ear that doth thy lays esteem
And gives thy pen both skill and argument.
Rise, resty Muse, my love's sweet face survey,
If Time have any wrinkle graven there.   10
If any, be a satire to decay
And make Time's spoils despised everywhere.
    Give my love fame faster than Time wastes life:
    So thou prevent'st his scythe and crooked knife.

SONNET 101. *2 truth* fidelity. *dy'd* stamped. *4 thou* the Muse. *dignified* you are dignified. *5 haply* perhaps. *6 Truth . . . fix'd* truth needs no artificial ornamentation since its colour is natural and permanent. *7 lay* lay on, apply. *8 intermix'd* adulterated with alien substance. *11 To make . . . gilded tomb* i.e. make him immortal by praising him in verse. *13 do thy office* perform your proper function. *14 shows* appears.

SONNET 102. *1 seeming* outward appearance. *2 appear* is evident. *3-4 That love . . . everywhere* that love is treated like a merchant's goods when he who possesses it publicly proclaims its value. *6 wont* accustomed. *7 Philomel* the nightingale. Although it is actually only the male nightingale who sings, the classical Philomela was a girl and is always treated by Shakespeare as feminine. *in summer's front* at the beginning of summer. *8 her* HAUSMAN; Q: "his." *pipe* voice. *in growth . . . days* as late summer comes. *11 But that . . . every bough* but because there are songbirds now singing in every tree. There is a quibble on "burden" in the sense of "refrain" of a song. *13 sometime* from time to time. *14 dull* cloy.

102

101

O truant Muse, what shall be thy amends
For thy neglect of truth in beauty dy'd?
Both truth and beauty on my love depends;
So dost thou too, and therein dignified.
Make answer, Muse. Wilt thou not haply say, 5
"Truth needs no colour, with his colour fix'd;
Beauty no pencil, beauty's truth to lay;
But best is best, if never intermix'd"?
Because he needs no praise, wilt thou be dumb?
Excuse not silence so; for't lies in thee 10
To make him much outlive a gilded tomb
And to be prais'd of ages yet to be.
    Then do thy office, Muse. I teach thee how
    To make him seem, long hence, as he shows now.

102

My love is strength'ned, though more weak in seeming;
I love not less, though less the show appear.
That love is merchandiz'd whose rich esteeming
The owner's tongue doth publish everywhere.
Our love was new, and then but in the spring, 5
When I was wont to greet it with my lays,
As Philomel in summer's front doth sing
And stops her pipe in growth of riper days;
Not that the summer is less pleasant now
Than when her mournful hymns did hush the night, 10
But that wild music burdens every bough,
And sweets grown common lose their dear delight.
    Therefore, like her, I sometime hold my tongue,
    Because I would not dull you with my song.

103

SONNET 103. *1 poverty* impoverished, inferior verse. *2 scope* free opportunity. *3 argument all bare* naked theme — you, without adornment. *6 glass* mirror. *7 overgoes . . . quite* surpasses my crude poetic creations completely. *8 Dulling my lines* making my verses seem trite and lifeless. *doing me disgrace* putting me to shame. *9 mend* improve upon (my beautiful subject). *11 pass* purpose. *13 sit* reside.

SONNET 104. The sonnet was apparently written three years after the poet first met his friend. Most editors regard it as misplaced in its present position in the sequence. *4 pride* glorious appearance. *6 process* the progress. *7 burn'd* i.e. like incense. *8 green* young, beautiful. *9 dial* clock. *10 his figure* the number on the face of the clock. *11 hue* complexion, appearance. *methinks . . . stand* seems to me never to be changing. *13 thou age unbred* The poet speaks directly to the future ages who will read his poem.

103

Alack, what poverty my Muse brings forth,
That, having such a scope to show her pride,
The argument all bare is of more worth
Than when it hath my added praise beside!
O, blame me not if I no more can write!   5
Look in your glass, and there appears a face
That overgoes my blunt invention quite,
Dulling my lines and doing me disgrace.
Were it not sinful then, striving to mend,
To mar the subject that before was well?   10
For to no other pass my verses tend
Than of your graces and your gifts to tell;
    And more, much more, than in my verse can sit
    Your own glass shows you when you look in it.

104

To me, fair friend, you never can be old,
For as you were when first your eye I ey'd,
Such seems your beauty still. Three winters cold
Have from the forests shook three summers' pride,
Three beauteous springs to yellow autumn turn'd   5
In process of the seasons have I seen,
Three April perfumes in three hot Junes burn'd,
Since first I saw you fresh, which yet are green.
Ah, yet doth beauty, like a dial hand,
Steal from his figure, and no pace perceiv'd!   10
So your sweet hue, which methinks still doth stand,
Hath motion, and mine eye may be deceiv'd;
    For fear of which, hear this, thou age unbred:
    Ere you were born was beauty's summer dead.

SONNET 105. *1 Let . . . idolatry* The poet's love is not idolatrous, he maintains, because it is directed to one god and is unchanging in its fidelity. *2 show* appear. *4 still* always, forever. *5 Kind* natural. *6 Still constant* always the same. *8 leaves out difference* avoids variety. *11 And in . . . invention spent* and in ringing changes on this theme all my poetic skill is expended. *14 kept seat* were lodged together.

SONNET 106. *1 wasted time* past ages. *2 wights* persons. *3 And beauty . . . old rhyme* and beautiful persons causing old poems about them to be beautiful. *5 blazon* trumpeting forth, celebration. *7 antique* ancient. *8 master* possess. *10 you prefiguring* foreshadowing you. *11 for* because. *divining eyes* eyes which look into the future. *12 skill* CAPELL; Q: "still."

106

105

Let not my love be call'd idolatry
Nor my beloved as an idol show,
Since all alike my songs and praises be
To one, of one, still such, and ever so.
Kind is my love to-day, to-morrow kind, 5
Still constant in a wondrous excellence;
Therefore my verse, to constancy confin'd,
One thing expressing, leaves out difference.
"Fair, kind, and true," is all my argument,
"Fair, kind, and true," varying to other words; 10
And in this change is my invention spent,
Three themes in one, which wondrous scope affords.
    Fair, kind, and true have often liv'd alone,
    Which three till now never kept seat in one.

106

When in the chronicle of wasted time
I see descriptions of the fairest wights,
And beauty making beautiful old rhyme
In praise of ladies dead and lovely knights,
Then, in the blazon of sweet beauty's best, 5
Of hand, of foot, of lip, of eye, of brow,
I see their antique pen would have express'd
Even such a beauty as you master now.
So all their praises are but prophecies
Of this our time, all you prefiguring; 10
And, for they look'd but with divining eyes,
They had not skill enough your worth to sing;
    For we, which now behold these present days,
    Have eyes to wonder, but lack tongues to praise.

107

SONNET 107. Since this sonnet seems to refer to specific events, it has been used perhaps more than any other in attempts to date the sequence. Just what events it refers to has been much debated. *1–4 Not mine . . . confin'd doom* not my own apprehensions nor the intuitive fears of the world at large can envisage an end to my love, supposedly limited by a fixed period of years (the fact of mortality). *5 The mortal . . . endur'd* This has been taken as an allusion to (a) the defeat in 1588 of the Spanish Armada, which sailed in a crescent formation (b) Queen Elizabeth's illness in 1599–1600, since she was commonly referred to as Diana or the moon (c) the death of the Queen in 1603. There have been many other suggestions. *6 sad augurs . . . presage* gloomy prophets now laugh at their own past predictions of disaster. Precisely what disasters they had predicted has also been a subject for much debate. *7 Incertainties . . . assur'd* a period of uncertainties has given way to one of confidence. *8 And peace . . . endless age* we may now look forward to a period of perpetual peace. Some have taken this as an allusion to the accession of James I and his attempts to end the long hostilities with Spain. *9 drops . . . time* The metaphor is of healing rainfall. *10 to me subscribes* acknowledges me as its superior. *12 insults o'er* haughtily triumphs over. *dull . . . tribes* the common inarticulate multitude. *14 are spent* have perished.

SONNET 108. *1 character* write. *2 figur'd* revealed. *3 register* record. *8 hallowed* made holy. *9 in love's fresh case* in the young exterior embodiment of love. *10 Weighs* values. *11 place* consideration. *12 for aye his page* his servant forever. *13 conceit* conception.

Not mine own fears, nor the prophetic soul
Of the wide world, dreaming on things to come,
Can yet the lease of my true love control,
Suppos'd as forfeit to a confin'd doom.
The mortal moon hath her eclipse endur'd,   5
And the sad augurs mock their own presage;
Incertainties now crown themselves assur'd,
And peace proclaims olives of endless age.
Now with the drops of this most balmy time
My love looks fresh, and Death to me subscribes,   10
Since, spite of him, I'll live in this poor rhyme
While he insults o'er dull and speechless tribes;
    And thou in this shalt find thy monument
    When tyrants' crests and tombs of brass are spent.

What's in the brain that ink may character
Which hath not figur'd to thee my true spirit?
What's new to speak, what new to register,
That may express my love or thy dear merit?
Nothing, sweet boy; but yet, like prayers divine,   5
I must each day say o'er the very same;
Counting no old thing old, thou mine, I thine,
Even as when first I hallowed thy fair name.
So that eternal love in love's fresh case
Weighs not the dust and injury of age,   10
Nor gives to necessary wrinkles place,
But makes antiquity for aye his page,
    Finding the first conceit of love there bred
    Where time and outward form would show it dead.

SONNET 109. *2 my flame to qualify* to abate my passion. *5 rang'd* wandered, been inconstant. *7 Just to . . . exchang'd* punctual and unaltered by the time (of separation). *8 bring . . . stain* wipe out my guilt with tears (water) of repentance. *10 all kinds of blood* persons of every kind of passion. *11 preposterously* unnaturally. *12 for* in exchange for. *14 in it* in "this wide universe."

SONNET 110. *2 a motley to the view* a jester on public display. Some critics have seen in this sonnet evidence of Shakespeare's distaste for his profession as an actor. *3 Gor'd* wounded. *4 Made old . . . new* turned new friendships into occasions for my old offence of inconstancy. *5 truth* fidelity, constancy. *6 Askance* with indifference. *strangely* as though I were a stranger to it. *7 blenches* disdainful looks, sidelong glances. *gave . . . youth* rejuvenated my love for you. *8 worse essays* experiences with inferior friendships. *10–11 Mine appetite . . . older friend* I will never sharpen my appetite for love by experimenting with new friends so as to prove the value of an older friend. *12 confin'd* bound. *13 my heaven* i.e. your breast. It is doubtful that the expression is one of Christian piety, as some have supposed.

110

O, never say that I was false of heart,
Though absence seem'd my flame to qualify!
As easy might I from myself depart
As from my soul, which in thy breast doth lie.
That is my home of love. If I have rang'd,   5
Like him that travels I return again,
Just to the time, not with the time exchang'd,
So that myself bring water for my stain.
Never believe, though in my nature reign'd
All frailties that besiege all kinds of blood,   10
That it could so preposterously be stain'd
To leave for nothing all thy sum of good;
    For nothing this wide universe I call
    Save thou, my rose; in it thou art my all.

Alas, 'tis true I have gone here and there
And made myself a motley to the view,
Gor'd mine own thoughts, sold cheap what is most
    dear,
Made old offences of affections new.
Most true it is that I have look'd on truth   5
Askance and strangely; but, by all above,
These blenches gave my heart another youth,
And worse essays prov'd thee my best of love.
Now all is done, have what shall have no end!
Mine appetite I never more will grind   10
On newer proof, to try an older friend,
A god in love, to whom I am confin'd.
    Then give me welcome, next my heaven the best,
    Even to thy pure and most most loving breast.

SONNET 111. *1 with* GILDON; Q: "wish." *chide* quarrel. *2 of* responsible for. *4 public means* the necessity to appear in public (as an actor). *public manners breeds* gives rise to vulgar manners. *5 brand* stigma. *6–7 And almost . . . dyer's hand* and because of that my nature, like the dyer's hand, is almost coloured by the material it must work with. *8 renew'd* cleansed. *10 eysell* vinegar (prescribed by some physicians to prevent the plague). *11–12 No bitterness . . . correct correction* I will consider no bitter remedy to be bitter and I will undergo double penance to cure my ill behaviour.

SONNET 112. *1 th' impression fill* remove the scar. *2 vulgar* common. *stamp'd . . . brow* The allusion is to the branding of criminals upon the forehead. *3 calls . . . ill* gives me a good reputation or a bad one. *4 So you . . . good allow* so long as you cover over what is bad in me and acknowledge what is good. To "o'er-green" is to cover a bare spot of ground with grass. *7–8 None else . . . or wrong* no other person exists who can change my fixed sense of what is either right or wrong. This is the general meaning of these obscure lines which have been much debated and often emended. *9 profound* deep. *10 voices* opinions. *adder's sense* deaf ears. The adder was believed to be deaf. *12 Mark how . . . do dispense* see how I excuse my refusal to hear (other people's opinions). *13 strongly . . . bred* firmly centered in all my thoughts and concerns. *14 methinks are* CAPELL; Q: "me thinkes y'are."

111

O, for my sake do you with Fortune chide,
The guilty goddess of my harmful deeds,
That did not better for my life provide
Than public means which public manners breeds.
Thence comes it that my name receives a brand;   5
And almost thence my nature is subdu'd
To what it works in, like the dyer's hand.
Pity me then, and wish I were renew'd,
Whilst, like a willing patient, I will drink
Potions of eysell 'gainst my strong infection;   10
No bitterness that I will bitter think,
Nor double penance, to correct correction.
    Pity me, then, dear friend, and I assure ye
    Even that your pity is enough to cure me.

112

Your love and pity doth th' impression fill
Which vulgar scandal stamp'd upon my brow;
For what care I who calls me well or ill,
So you o'er-green my bad, my good allow?
You are my all the world, and I must strive   5
To know my shames and praises from your tongue —
None else to me, nor I to none alive,
That my steel'd sense or changes right or wrong.
In so profound abysm I throw all care
Of others' voices that my adder's sense   10
To critic and to flatterer stopped are.
Mark how with my neglect I do dispense:
    You are so strongly in my purpose bred
    That all the world besides methinks are dead.

SONNET 113. *1 mine eye . . . mind* I can see only your image in my mind. *2–4 And that . . . is out* and that (my eye) which directs my steps abandons his duty, and although seeming to see is actually blind. *5 form* impression, image. *6 latch* catch sight of (MALONE; Q: "lack"). *7 Of his . . . no part* the mind does not share in its (the eye's) fleeting visions. *8 Nor his . . . doth catch* nor does the eye retain what is caught within its view. *9 rud'st* most uncouth. *gentlest* most noble. *10 favour* appearance. *12 to your feature* so as to resemble your form. *13 Incapable of* unable to receive. *14 true* faithful. *mak'th mine eye* LETTSOM; Q: "maketh mine vntrue."

SONNET 114. *1 crown'd with you* filled with the joy of possessing you. *4 alchemy* transformation (of lesser sights into your appearance, as the alchemist transforms base metals into gold). *5 things indigest* shapeless things. *6 cherubins* angelic shapes. *8 As fast . . . assemble* It was believed that the eye gave forth beams; objects became visible when they were touched by these beams. *10 great* full. *most kingly* Flattery was the vice to which kings were believed most susceptible. *11 what with . . . greeing* what is most agreeable to the taste of my mind. *12 to his . . . cup* tastes from the cup as a king's official taster was required to do. *13–14 'tis the . . . first begin* the eye's sin is the less in that he has given the mind something he himself has tasted and enjoyed.

114

113

Since I left you, mine eye is in my mind;
And that which governs me to go about
Doth part his function and is partly blind,
Seems seeing, but effectually is out;
For it no form delivers to the heart   5
Of bird, of flow'r, or shape which it doth latch;
Of his quick objects hath the mind no part,
Nor his own vision holds what it doth catch;
For if it see the rud'st or gentlest sight,
The most sweet favour or deformed'st creature,   10
The mountain or the sea, the day or night,
The crow or dove, it shapes them to your feature.
  Incapable of more, replete with you,
  My most true mind thus mak'th mine eye untrue.

114

Or whether doth my mind, being crown'd with you,
Drink up the monarch's plague, this flattery?
Or whether shall I say mine eye saith true,
And that your love taught it this alchemy,
To make of monsters and things indigest   5
Such cherubins as your sweet self resemble,
Creating every bad a perfect best
As fast as objects to his beams assemble?
O, 'tis the first! 'Tis flatt'ry in my seeing,
And my great mind most kingly drinks it up.   10
Mine eye well knows what with his gust is greeing,
And to his palate doth prepare the cup.
  If it be poison'd, 'tis the lesser sin
  That mine eye loves it and doth first begin.

SONNET 115. *5 But reckoning Time* but when I consider Time. *whose million'd accidents* whose passing events are numbered by the millions. *6 Creep in 'twixt* interfere with. *7 Tan* take the freshness of youth from. *blunt* turn aside. *8 Divert strong . . . alt'ring things* turn determined minds away from their purposes and cause them to accept things as they change. *11 o'er incertainty* beyond the possibility of doubt. *12 Crowning* glorifying. *doubting of the rest* doubting whether the future could ever equal the present. *13-14 Then might . . . doth grow* at that time I could not say "Now I love you best," for that would have been to treat as fully mature a love which, like a baby, was continually growing.

SONNET 116. *1 marriage . . . minds* the perfect union of faithful minds. The poet is presenting a definition of perfect friendship. *2 impediments* There is an echo of the marriage service in the Book of Common Prayer: "If any of you know cause, or just impediment, why these two persons should not be joined together in holy matrimony, ye are to declare it." *3 alteration* (a) infidelity (b) impairment of beauty by the ravages of time. *4 bends . . . remove* inclines to stop loving when the loved person is unfaithful. *5 mark* sea-mark. *7 wand'ring bark* lost ship. *8 Whose worth's unknown* whose value is so great that it cannot be calculated. *his height be taken* its (the star's) altitude be measured (as with a sextant). *9 Time's fool* subservient to and controlled by Time. *10 Within . . . come* come within (and are thus mowed down by) the sweep of Time's curved scythe. *11 his* Time's. *12 bears it out* endures defiantly. *doom* doomsday. *13-14 If this . . . ever loved* if what I have just said about love is wrong and my error is demonstrated by my own case, then I have never written anything and no man's love has ever been real love.

✧✧✧✧✧✧✧✧ 115

Those lines that I before have writ do lie,
Even those that said I could not love you dearer.
Yet then my judgment knew no reason why
My most full flame should afterwards burn clearer.
But reckoning Time, whose million'd accidents   5
Creep in 'twixt vows and change decrees of kings,
Tan sacred beauty, blunt the sharp'st intents,
Divert strong minds to th' course of alt'ring things —
Alas, why, fearing of Time's tyranny,
Might I not then say "Now I love you best"   10
When I was certain o'er incertainty,
Crowning the present, doubting of the rest?
   Love is a babe. Then might I not say so,
   To give full growth to that which still doth grow.

✧✧✧✧✧✧✧✧ 116

Let me not to the marriage of true minds
Admit impediments. Love is not love
Which alters when it alteration finds
Or bends with the remover to remove.
O, no! it is an ever-fixed mark   5
That looks on tempests and is never shaken;
It is the star to every wand'ring bark,
Whose worth's unknown, although his height be
    taken.
Love's not Time's fool, though rosy lips and cheeks
Within his bending sickle's compass come.   10
Love alters not with his brief hours and weeks,
But bears it out even to the edge of doom.
   If this be error, and upon me proved,
   I never writ, nor no man ever loved.

117

SONNET 117. *1–2 that I . . . deserts repay* that I have neglected to do all the things which your great merits required of me. *3 upon . . . to call* to invoke your most precious love (as in religious worship). *4 bonds* (a) obligations (b) ties of friendship. *6 given . . . right* wasted my time which rightfully I should have devoted to you, since you have paid for it dearly with your friendship. *7–8 That I . . . your sight* I have given way to every passing distraction which was likely to remove me from your sight. *9 Book* record. *10 on just . . . accumulate* pile suspicions on top of what you can prove as certain. *11 level* aim. *13 my appeal* my plea in my defence. *14 virtue* strength.

SONNET 118. *1 Like as* just as. *2 With eager . . . urge* we stimulate our appetites with sharp sauces. *3 As* just as. *prevent* forestall. *unseen* whose symptoms may not yet be seen. *4 We sicken . . . purge* we make ourselves sick when we take laxatives so as to prevent sickness. Some critics have been offended by the medical imagery. *6 To bitter . . . feeding* i.e. associated with inferior persons. *7 sick of welfare* being overfed with happiness. *7–8 found a kind . . . true needing* found it appropriate to become sick before it was really necessary. *9 policy* trickery, cunning strategy. *anticipate* provide against. *10 faults assured* actual illnesses. *12 rank of* too full of (a medical term). *14 so* in that manner.

117

Accuse me thus: that I have scanted all
Wherein I should your great deserts repay;
Forgot upon your dearest love to call,
Whereto all bonds do tie me day by day;
That I have frequent been with unknown minds   5
And given to time your own dear-purchas'd right;
That I have hoisted sail to all the winds
Which should transport me farthest from your sight.
Book both my wilfulness and errors down,
And on just proof surmise accumulate;   10
Bring me within the level of your frown,
But shoot not at me in your wakened hate;
    Since my appeal says I did strive to prove
    The constancy and virtue of your love.

118

Like as, to make our appetites more keen,
With eager compounds we our palate urge;
As, to prevent our maladies unseen,
We sicken to shun sickness when we purge:
Even so, being full of your ne'er-cloying sweetness,   5
To bitter sauces did I frame my feeding;
And, sick of welfare, found a kind of meetness
To be diseas'd ere that there was true needing.
Thus policy in love, t' anticipate
The ills that were not, grew to faults assured,   10
And brought to medicine a healthful state,
Which, rank of goodness, would by ill be cured.
    But thence I learn, and find the lesson true,
    Drugs poison him that so fell sick of you.

119

SONNET 119. *1 Siren tears* tears of a temptress. The reference may be to the "dark lady" or to various women with whom the poet has associated. *2 limbecks* alembics, stills. *3 Applying* i.e. as medicine is applied. *4 Still losing . . . to win* always losing what I expected to gain. *6 so blessed never* ever so blessed. *7–8 How have . . . madding fever* how my eyes have started out of their sockets in the delirium of my maddening fever. *10 That better . . . made better* that superior things are always improved after they have been brought into contact with evil. *13 to my content* to my true friend, my source of contentment. *14 spent* wasted.

SONNET 120. *2–3 for that . . . transgression bow* because of the sorrow I felt when you were unkind to me, I am now overwhelmed by my sense of the wrong I have done to you. *4 nerves* sinews. *8 weigh* consider. *in your crime* because of your offence against me. *9 rememb'red* reminded. *11 tend'red* offered. *13–14 that your trespass . . . ransom me* that offence of yours has become the payment which I can offer you in expiation for my own offence against you.

What potions have I drunk of Siren tears,
Distill'd from limbecks foul as hell within,
Applying fears to hopes and hopes to fears,
Still losing when I saw myself to win!
What wretched errors hath my heart committed   5
Whilst it hath thought itself so blessed never!
How have mine eyes out of their spheres been fitted
In the distraction of this madding fever!
O benefit of ill! Now I find true
That better is by evil still made better;   10
And ruin'd love, when it is built anew,
Grows fairer than at first, more strong, far greater.
  So I return rebuk'd to my content,
  And gain by ills thrice more than I have spent.

That you were once unkind befriends me now,
And for that sorrow which I then did feel
Needs must I under my transgression bow,
Unless my nerves were brass or hammered steel.
For if you were by my unkindness shaken,   5
As I by yours, y'have pass'd a hell of time,
And I, a tyrant, have no leisure taken
To weigh how once I suffered in your crime.
O that our night of woe might have rememb'red
My deepest sense how hard true sorrow hits,   10
And soon to you, as you to me then, tend'red
The humble salve which wounded bosoms fits!
  But that your trespass now becomes a fee;
  Mine ransoms yours, and yours must ransom me.

SONNET 121. *1–2 'Tis better . . . of being* it is better to be truly vile than to be considered vile unjustly, when one who is not vile receives all of the reproach due to one who is. *3–4 And the just . . . others' seeing* and that proper pleasure is lost which is considered vile not by us who experience it but by others who view it from the outside. *5–6 For why . . . sportive blood* why should the prurient eyes of others hail my sexual passion (as akin to their own)? *7 frailties* human faults. *are frailer spies* are there more faulty observers. *8 in their wills* (a) wilfully (b) according to their own lustful feelings. *9 am that* am what. *level* take aim. *10 abuses* transgressions. *11 bevel* crooked. *12 rank* gross, sensual. *14 reign* exercise authority, pass judgment.

SONNET 122. *1 tables* notebook. *2 character'd* inscribed. *3 idle rank* empty leaves. *4 Beyond all date* longer than time itself. *6 Have faculty . . . to subsist* are permitted by nature to exist. *7 raz'd oblivion* oblivion which obliterates all things. *his* its. *8 miss'd* lost. *9 poor retention* inadequate container (the leaves of the "tables"). *10 tallies* sticks on which totals were "scored" by notching. *11–12 to give . . . thee more* I had the temerity to give them (the "tables") away so that I could rely upon my memory ("those tables") which is capable of more adequately recording my love for you. *13 adjunct* aid, such as a notebook. *14 import* imply.

'Tis better to be vile than vile esteemed
When not to be receives reproach of being,
And the just pleasure lost, which is so deemed
Not by our feeling but by others' seeing.
For why should others' false adulterate eyes   5
Give salutation to my sportive blood?
Or on my frailties why are frailer spies,
Which in their wills count bad what I think good?
No, I am that I am; and they that level
At my abuses reckon up their own.   10
I may be straight though they themselves be bevel;
By their rank thoughts my deeds must not be shown,
   Unless this general evil they maintain —
   All men are bad and in their badness reign.

Thy gift, thy tables, are within my brain
Full character'd with lasting memory,
Which shall above that idle rank remain
Beyond all date, even to eternity;
Or, at the least, so long as brain and heart   5
Have faculty by nature to subsist,
Till each to raz'd oblivion yield his part
Of thee, thy record never can be miss'd.
That poor retention could not so much hold,
Nor need I tallies thy dear love to score.   10
Therefore to give them from me was I bold,
To trust those tables that receive thee more.
   To keep an adjunct to remember thee
   Were to import forgetfulness in me.

SONNET 123. *2 pyramids* obelisks, memorial columns. Various attempts have been made to identify the specific memorials referred to and thus to date the sonnet. Some suggestions include those brought to Rome by Pope Sixtus V around 1585 and those erected to celebrate the entry of King James I into London on March 15, 1604. *4 dressings . . . sight* imitations of what has been seen before. *5 dates* lives. *admire* wonder at. *6 foist . . . old* pass off on us as new that is really old. *7 make . . . desire* regard them as newly created to our taste. *9 registers* historical records. *11 thy records . . . doth lie* both the records of the past and what we see in the present misrepresent reality. *12 Made more . . . continual haste* appearing either disproportionately large or small because of the rapidity with which you (Time) move. *14 true* faithful.

SONNET 124. *1 dear love* sincere passion (for his friend). *the child of state* controlled by either (a) political circumstances or (b) the wealth and position of the loved one. *2 for . . . unfather'd* as merely the bastard of Fortune be without a real father. *3-4 As subject . . . flowers gather'd* If his love were merely the bastard of Fortune, the poet is saying, it would be subject to Time's whims, a weed among weeds when Time hated it or a flower among flowers when Time loved it. *5 accident* chance occurrence. *6 suffers not* does not deteriorate. *7 thralled* oppressive. *8 Whereto . . . calls* to which the temptations of our time expose us all. *9 Policy* political cunning, expediency. *10 Which works . . . hours* which operates only in terms of short-range considerations (whereas love is eternal). *11 hugely politic* supremely prudent. Love is the only true "policy." *12 That it nor* since it neither. *grows . . . show'rs* i.e. is affected by fair weather or by foul. *13 fools of time* time-servers, subject to the control of time. *14 Which die . . . for crime* Allusion to specific malefactors who died repentant has been suspected in the line. Various suggestions have included the Earl of Essex and his followers, the perpetrators of the Gunpowder Plot, Catholic priests executed in 1594 and 1595, and the dramatists Marlowe, Peele and Greene.

◇◇◇◇◇◇◇◇◇ 123

No, Time, thou shalt not boast that I do change!
Thy pyramids built up with newer might
To me are nothing novel, nothing strange;
They are but dressings of a former sight.
Our dates are brief, and therefore we admire   5
What thou dost foist upon us that is old,
And rather make them born to our desire
Than think that we before have heard them told.
Thy registers and thee I both defy,
Not wond'ring at the present nor the past;   10
For thy records and what we see doth lie,
Made more or less by thy continual haste.
   This I do vow, and this shall ever be —
   I will be true, despite thy scythe and thee.

◇◇◇◇◇◇◇◇◇ 124

If my dear love were but the child of state,
It might for Fortune's bastard be unfather'd,
As subject to Time's love or to Time's hate,
Weeds among weeds, or flowers with flowers gather'd.
No, it was builded far from accident;   5
It suffers not in smiling pomp, nor falls
Under the blow of thralled discontent,
Whereto th' inviting time our fashion calls.
It fears not Policy, that heretic
Which works on leases of short-numb'red hours,   10
But all alone stands hugely politic,
That it nor grows with heat nor drowns with show'rs.
   To this I witness call the fools of time,
   Which die for goodness, who have liv'd for crime.

125

SONNET 125. *1 Were't aught to me* would it be of any advantage to me if. *bore the canopy* Canopies were held over kings and nobles on ceremonial occasions. Various specific events at which Shakespeare might have held up a canopy have been suggested, none very convincingly. *2 With my . . . honouring* by my external actions honouring external qualities. *3–4 Or laid . . . or ruining* or created the bases for eternal fame (the poems he has written) which proves to be briefer than time devoted to waste and extravagance. *proves* Q; MALONE, K: "prove." *5 dwellers . . . favour* those who overvalue mere outward appearance (with a pun on the sense of "tenants"). *6 Lose all . . . much rent* lose their patron's love by paying excessive tribute to his external features. *7 For compound . . . savour* for the compounded sweets (of high position and external beauty) give up the simple taste (of experiencing true love). *8 Pitiful thrivers . . . gazing spent* those who thrive poorly because they give up all for the sake of merely gazing at the one they love — like courtiers looking upon a king for preferment and receiving nothing. *9 let me . . . thy heart* let my true duty be felt in your heart (rather than displayed in outward show). *10 oblation* offering. *free* freely given. *11 mix'd with seconds* adulterated with baser matter. *knows no art* is without artifice. *12 mutual . . . for thee* exchange of my true self for your true self. *13 suborn'd informer* false witness. If there was an actual informer against the poet, he has not been identified. *14 impeach'd* accused.

SONNET 126. These twelve lines in rhymed couplets provide an envoy to the sonnets written by the poet to his friend. The remaining sonnets are addressed to his mistress. *1–2 in thy power . . . sickle, hour* Youth holds three aspects of time in his power: the mirror in which man sees his beauty fade, the sickle and the hourglass. *3–4 Who hast . . . self grow'st* who has (paradoxically) grown in beauty with time's passage and thus by contrast revealed the aging of your friends. *5 wrack* ruin, decay. *6 still* always. *8 disgrace* render ignominious. *9 fear* distrust. *minion* darling. *10 still* forever. *11–12 Her audit . . . render thee* Nature must eventually render her account to Time, and she can only make her settlement by surrendering you.

126

✧✧✧✧✧✧✧✧✧ 125

Were't aught to me I bore the canopy,
With my extern the outward honouring,
Or laid great bases for eternity,
Which proves more short than waste or ruining?
Have I not seen dwellers on form and favour   5
Lose all, and more, by paying too much rent,
For compound sweet forgoing simple savour —
Pitiful thrivers, in their gazing spent?
No, let me be obsequious in thy heart,
And take thou my oblation, poor but free,   10
Which is not mix'd with seconds, knows no art
But mutual render, only me for thee.
   Hence, thou suborn'd informer! A true soul
   When most impeach'd stands least in thy control.

✧✧✧✧✧✧✧✧✧ 126

O thou, my lovely boy, who in thy power
Dost hold Time's fickle glass, his sickle, hour;
Who hast by waning grown, and therein show'st
Thy lovers withering as thy sweet self grow'st —
If Nature (sovereign mistress over wrack),   5
As thou goest onwards, still will pluck thee back,
She keeps thee to this purpose, that her skill
May time disgrace, and wretched minutes kill.
Yet fear her, O thou minion of her pleasure!
She may detain, but not still keep, her treasure;   10
   Her audit, though delay'd, answer'd must be,
   And her quietus is to render thee.

SONNET 127. *1 the old age* former times. In chivalric romances only blonde women were considered beautiful, and this tradition survived in the sonnets of Shakespeare's contemporaries. *counted fair* considered beautiful (with a pun on "fair" in the sense of "blonde"). *3 successive heir* heir by right of succession. *4 And beauty . . . shame* and blonde beauty is declared illegitimate (as supposedly the product of cosmetics). *5-6 For since . . . borrow'd face* because everybody has assumed nature's power and is making ugly faces beautiful by painting them. *7-8 Sweet beauty . . . in disgrace* true beauty has lost its identity and dwelling place and is either profanely imitated or entirely discredited. *9 brows* STAUNTON; Q: "eyes." *10 so suited* similarly dressed, also black. *11 not born . . . lack* although not born blonde have acquired beauty by artificial means. *12 false esteem* false appearance of beauty. *13 becoming of* adorning, gracing.

SONNET 128. *1 thou, my music* you, who please me as music does. *2 blessed wood* the wooden keys of the virginal or spinet, made blessed by your touch. *3-4 gently sway'st . . . ear confounds* gently control the harmony of strings which amazes my ear with delight. *5 jacks* keys. *10 chips* keys. *11 thy* GILDON; Q: "their." *13 happy* fortunate. *14 thy* GILDON; Q: "their."

127

In the old age black was not counted fair,
Or if it were, it bore not beauty's name;
But now is black beauty's successive heir,
And beauty slander'd with a bastard shame;
For since each hand hath put on nature's power,   5
Fairing the foul with art's false borrow'd face,
Sweet beauty hath no name, no holy bower,
But is profan'd, if not lives in disgrace.
Therefore my mistress' brows are raven black,
Her eyes so suited, and they mourners seem   10
At such who, not born fair, no beauty lack,
Sland'ring creation with a false esteem.
    Yet so they mourn, becoming of their woe,
    That every tongue says beauty should look so.

128

How oft, when thou, my music, music play'st
Upon that blessed wood whose motion sounds
With thy sweet fingers when thou gently sway'st
The wiry concord that mine ear confounds,
Do I envy those jacks that nimble leap   5
To kiss the tender inward of thy hand,
Whilst my poor lips, which should that harvest reap,
At the wood's boldness by thee blushing stand!
To be so tickled, they would change their state
And situation with those dancing chips   10
O'er whom thy fingers walk with gentle gait,
Making dead wood more blest than living lips.
    Since saucy jacks so happy are in this,
    Give them thy fingers, me thy lips to kiss.

SONNET 129. *1 Th' expense . . . shame* the using up of vital spirits in a shameful act. *2 till action* until it is expressed in action. *3 full of blame* (a) harmful (b) guilty. *4 extreme* violent. *rude* brutal. *to trust* to be trusted. *10 quest* pursuit. *11 in proof* when experienced. *prov'd, a* MALONE; Q: "proud and." *14 the heaven* (a) the sensation of bliss (b) the woman who provides it.

SONNET 130. While the poet burlesques the elegant hyperboles of contemporary Petrarchan sonnets, he at the same time affirms his love for his mistress in spite of her failure to conform to the impossible ideal of the sonneteers. *1 nothing* not at all. *3 dun* dark. *4 If hairs be wires* Comparison of a lady's hair to the fine golden wire used by Florentine goldsmiths in filigree work was conventional. *5 damask'd* variegated (mingled red and white). *8 reeks* is exhaled. The verb did not have its present connotation of distaste. *11 go* walk. *12 treads on the ground* walks on the earth, like any other mortal woman. *13 love* mistress. *rare* beautiful, splendid. *14 As any . . . compare* as any other woman who is lied about by means of impossible comparisons.

129

Th' expense of spirit in a waste of shame
Is lust in action; and till action, lust
Is perjur'd, murd'rous, bloody, full of blame,
Savage, extreme, rude, cruel, not to trust;
Enjoy'd no sooner but despised straight;   5
Past reason hunted, and no sooner had,
Past reason hated, as a swallowed bait
On purpose laid to make the taker mad;
Mad in pursuit, and in possession so;
Had, having, and in quest to have, extreme;   10
A bliss in proof — and prov'd, a very woe;
Before, a joy propos'd; behind, a dream.
  All this the world well knows; yet none knows well
  To shun the heaven that leads men to this hell.

130

My mistress' eyes are nothing like the sun;
Coral is far more red than her lips' red;
If snow be white, why then her breasts are dun;
If hairs be wires, black wires grow on her head.
I have seen roses damask'd, red and white,   5
But no such roses see I in her cheeks;
And in some perfumes is there more delight
Than in the breath that from my mistress reeks.
I love to hear her speak; yet well I know
That music hath a far more pleasing sound.   10
I grant I never saw a goddess go:
My mistress, when she walks, treads on the ground.
  And yet, by heaven, I think my love as rare
  As any she belied with false compare.

SONNET 131. *1 so as thou art* being as you are (without such beauty as is conventionally praised). *2 whose beauties . . . cruel* who are made cruel through pride they feel in their beauties. *3 dear doting* (a) tenderly loving beyond reason (b) foolishly loving to my own cost. *7 To say* to assert publicly. *10 but thinking on* when I merely think of. *11 One . . . neck* in quick succession. *12 in my judgment's place* in the position which my judgment assigns to it. *14 this slander* i.e. that of line 6.

SONNET 132. *2 torments* WALKER; Q: "torment." *4 ruth* pity. *6 becomes* adorns. *8 Doth* renders. *9 mourning* GILDON; Q: "morning." Probably both meanings are intended. *10 as well* also. *beseem* be fitting for. *11 doth thee grace* makes you beautiful. *12 And suit . . . every part* and dress your pity (in black mourning) like the rest of you. *14 they* i.e. other women. *foul* ugly.

131

Thou art as tyrannous, so as thou art,
As those whose beauties proudly make them cruel;
For well thou know'st to my dear doting heart
Thou art the fairest and most precious jewel.
Yet, in good faith, some say that thee behold,　　　5
Thy face hath not the power to make love groan.
To say they err I dare not be so bold,
Although I swear it to myself alone.
And, to be sure that is not false I swear,
A thousand groans, but thinking on thy face,　　　10
One on another's neck, do witness bear
Thy black is fairest in my judgment's place.
　　In nothing art thou black save in thy deeds,
　　And thence this slander, as I think, proceeds.

132

Thine eyes I love, and they, as pitying me,
Knowing thy heart torments me with disdain,
Have put on black and loving mourners be,
Looking with pretty ruth upon my pain.
And truly not the morning sun of heaven　　　5
Better becomes the grey cheeks of the East,
Nor that full star that ushers in the even
Doth half that glory to the sober West,
As those two mourning eyes become thy face.
O, let it then as well beseem thy heart　　　10
To mourn for me, since mourning doth thee grace,
And suit thy pity like in every part.
　　Then will I swear beauty herself is black
　　And all they foul that thy complexion lack.

SONNET 133. *1 Beshrew* curse (in a mild sense). *4 slave to slavery* enslaved to the enslaved condition of his friend. *5 Me from . . . taken* your cruel eye has taken me away from my own true self. *6 And my . . . hast engrossed* and my true friend you have even more securely captured to keep entirely for yourself. *8 crossed* thwarted, afflicted. *9 ward* guarded cell. The notion of the lover's heart as imprisoned in the bosom of his mistress is a conventional one. *10 my friend's . . . bail* let my heart free my friend's heart by serving as your prisoner in its place. *11 keeps me* holds me prisoner. *his* my friend's. *guard* protector. *12 Thou canst . . . my jail* you cannot then make my imprisonment seem severe to me. *13 pent* locked up. *14 Perforce* (a) by force (b) of necessity. *in me* in my heart — i.e. my friend, whom you thus imprison also by imprisoning me.

SONNET 134. The sonnet plays on the double meanings of legal terms relating to the lending of money. *1 now* now that. *2 mortgag'd to thy will* pledged to satisfy your lust (and liable to forfeiture if I do not). *3 so* on condition that. *that other mine* my friend. *4 restore* give back. *still* in the future. *5 wilt not* will not give him back to me. *6 kind* (a) compliant (b) natural — in his sexual desires. *7–8 He learn'd . . . doth bind* he was merely taught to underwrite, as my surety, my bond of indebtedness to you, which now binds him as securely as it binds me. *9 The statute . . . wilt take* you will take the full forfeiture (both my friend and me) provided for by the bond which is your beauty (and the enjoyment of it). *10 put'st . . . use* who will lay out no part of your beauty except at interest. *11 came* who became. *12 my unkind abuse* your cruel deception of me. *14 He pays . . . not free* although he pays the entire debt (satisfies your lust completely) I am still not free from my obligation to you.

134

133

Beshrew that heart that makes my heart to groan
For that deep wound it gives my friend and me!
Is't not enough to torture me alone
But slave to slavery my sweet'st friend must be?
Me from myself thy cruel eye hath taken,   5
And my next self thou harder hast engrossed.
Of him, myself, and thee I am forsaken —
A torment thrice threefold thus to be crossed.
Prison my heart in thy steel bosom's ward;
But then my friend's heart let my poor heart bail;   10
Whoe'er keeps me, let my heart be his guard:
Thou canst not then use rigour in my jail.
    And yet thou wilt; for I, being pent in thee,
    Perforce am thine, and all that is in me.

134

So, now I have confess'd that he is thine
And I myself am mortgag'd to thy will,
Myself I'll forfeit, so that other mine
Thou wilt restore to be my comfort still.
But thou wilt not, nor he will not be free,   5
For thou art covetous, and he is kind;
He learn'd but surety-like to write for me
Under that bond that him as fast doth bind.
The statute of thy beauty thou wilt take,
Thou usurer that put'st forth all to use,   10
And sue a friend came debtor for my sake:
So him I lose through my unkind abuse.
    Him have I lost, thou hast both him and me:
    He pays the whole, and yet am I not free.

SONNET 135. In this and the following sonnet the poet plays on various meanings of the word "Will" (a) his own name, and possibly the name of his friend and the name of the lady's husband (b) lust or carnal desire (c) wilfulness, volition (d) the male or female genitals. Where the word is capitalized in the present text it is both capitalized and italicized in Q. *2 to boot* in addition. *Will in overplus* an extra Will. Perhaps the poet means himself, the others being his friend and the lady's husband. *3 still* always. *4 To thy . . . addition thus* adding myself to what you sweetly desire. *6 vouchsafe* consent. *hide . . . thine* i.e. grant me fulfilment of my sexual desires. *9 still* continually. *13 unkind* refusal (on your part). *fair beseechers* legitimate pleaders. *14 Think all . . . one Will* consider all your "Wills" as one corporate lover, and include me in that one "Will" — all the meanings of the word apparently being present in this final example of it.

SONNET 136. *1 check* rebuke. *come so near* (a) am so frank, in referring to your sexuality (b) come so close to your bed. *2 blind soul* deliberately unseeing soul (which should protect the lady's chastity). *3 will* carnal desire. *admitted* allowed to enter. *there* in your bedchamber. *4 fulfil* grant. *5-6 Will will . . . will one* The lines are coarsely sexual in their playing on the various meanings of "will." *7 receipt* capacity. *prove* know from experience. *8 Among . . . none* a single item in a large quantity is not considered significant. *9 untold* uncounted. *10 Though in . . . must be* although I do increase the total number of your lovers. *11 For nothing hold me* regard me as of no consequence. *so it please thee* so long as it pleases thee to. *13 my name* i.e. will, in the sense of carnal desire. *14 for* because.

135

Whoever hath her wish, thou hast thy Will,
And Will to boot, and Will in overplus.
More than enough am I that vex thee still,
To thy sweet will making addition thus.
Wilt thou, whose will is large and spacious,   5
Not once vouchsafe to hide my will in thine?
Shall will in others seem right gracious
And in my will no fair acceptance shine?
The sea, all water, yet receives rain still
And in abundance addeth to his store;   10
So thou, being rich in Will, add to thy Will
One will of mine to make thy large Will more.
    Let no unkind no fair beseechers kill;
    Think all but one, and me in that one Will.

136

If thy soul check thee that I come so near,
Swear to thy blind soul that I was thy Will,
And will, thy soul knows, is admitted there:
Thus far for love my love-suit, sweet, fulfil.
Will will fulfil the treasure of thy love,   5
Ay, fill it full with wills, and my will one.
In things of great receipt with ease we prove
Among a number one is reckon'd none.
Then in the number let me pass untold,
Though in thy store's account I one must be;   10
For nothing hold me, so it please thee hold
That nothing me, a something, sweet, to thee.
    Make but my name thy love, and love that still,
    And then thou lovest me for my name is Will.

SONNET 137. *1 Love* Cupid, the blind child of Venus. *3 lies* resides. *4 what . . . to be* take the worst to be the best — i.e. consider my false mistress to be beautiful. *5 corrupt* corrupted. *6 Be anchor'd . . . men ride* have caused me to be anchored in a common harbour. The bitter sexual implication is obvious. *7 falsehood* deception. *forged* created. *9 that a several plot* that place (woman) a private possession. *10 common* open to all. *11 not* not the case. *13-14 In things . . . transferred* The suggestion is that because the poet in the past has failed to recognize true love and beauty as a punishment his eyes and heart have now been afflicted with the plague of deception.

SONNET 138. *1 truth* (a) veracity (b) fidelity. *2 believe* pretend to believe. *lies* (a) prevaricates (b) fornicates. The poet is deliberately ambiguous. *3 That* in order that. *5 vainly* in self-deception. *7 Simply* (a) pretending to be simpleminded (b) completely, absolutely. *credit* believe. *9 unjust* unfaithful. *11 habit* appearance. *13 lie* Again used with deliberate ambiguity. *14 And in . . . flattered be* and in our respective shortcomings each of us is flattered by the lies of the other.

138

137

Thou blind fool, Love, what dost thou to mine eyes
That they behold, and see not what they see?
They know what beauty is, see where it lies,
Yet what the best is take the worst to be.
If eyes, corrupt by over-partial looks,   5
Be anchor'd in the bay where all men ride,
Why of eyes' falsehood hast thou forged hooks,
Whereto the judgment of my heart is tied?
Why should my heart think that a several plot
Which my heart knows the wide world's common
    place?   10
Or mine eyes seeing this, say this is not,
To put fair truth upon so foul a face?
  In things right true my heart and eyes have erred,
  And to this false plague are they now transferred.

138

When my love swears that she is made of truth
I do believe her, though I know she lies,
That she might think me some untutor'd youth,
Unlearned in the world's false subtilties.
Thus vainly thinking that she thinks me young,   5
Although she knows my days are past the best,
Simply I credit her false-speaking tongue:
On both sides thus is simple truth suppress'd.
But wherefore says she not she is unjust?
And wherefore say not I that I am old?   10
O, love's best habit is in seeming trust,
And age in love loves not to have years told.
  Therefore I lie with her and she with me,
  And in our faults by lies we flattered be.

139

SONNET 139. *1 O, call . . . the wrong* For the lover to find an excuse for his mistress's unkindness was a common convention of the love sonnet. *2 unkindness* cruelty, infidelity. *3 Wound me . . . thy tongue* do not make me see your infidelity; merely tell me about it. *4 Use power . . . by art* kill me directly with your full force and not by indirect contrived means. *5–6 but in . . . eye aside* but when you are with me restrain yourself from casting loving eyes upon another. *8 o'erpress'd . . . bide* overpowered defences can resist. *10 pretty* wanton, lascivious. *11 my foes* i.e. her eyes. *14 rid* quickly put an end to.

SONNET 140. *1 press* oppress. *4 pity-wanting* unpitied. *6 so* i.e. that you do love me. *7 testy* fretful. *8 know* are told. *11 ill-wresting* misinterpreting everything in an evil way. *12 mad ears* i.e. persons as ready to believe slander as I in my madness will be to slander you. *13 be so* be believed in that way. *belied* lied about. *14 go wide* go astray.

139

O, call not me to justify the wrong
That thy unkindness lays upon my heart!
Wound me not with thine eye, but with thy tongue;
Use power with power, and slay me not by art!
Tell me thou lov'st elsewhere; but in my sight,   5
Dear heart, forbear to glance thine eye aside.
What need'st thou wound with cunning when thy
. might
Is more than my o'erpress'd defence can bide?
Let me excuse thee: — Ah, my love well knows
Her pretty looks have been mine enemies;   10
And therefore from my face she turns my foes,
That they elsewhere might dart their injuries.
    Yet do not so; but since I am near slain,
    Kill me outright with looks and rid my pain.

140

Be wise as thou art cruel; do not press
My tongue-tied patience with too much disdain;
Lest sorrow lend me words, and words express
The manner of my pity-wanting pain.
If I might teach thee wit, better it were,   5
Though not to love, yet, love, to tell me so;
As testy sick men, when their deaths be near,
No news but health from their physicians know.
For if I should despair, I should grow mad,
And in my madness might speak ill of thee.   10
Now this ill-wresting world is grown so bad
Mad slanderers by mad ears believed be.
    That I may not be so, nor thou belied,
    Bear thine eyes straight, though thy proud heart go
    wide.

SONNET 141. *2 errors* defects. *4 Who* which. *despite of view* in spite of what can be seen. *6 Nor tender . . . prone* nor my delicate sense of feeling inclined to respond to any ordinary common touch (it requires something more rarified). *8 alone* in particular (and not with other women as well). *9 But my* but neither my. *five wits* These were defined by Stephen Hawes, THE PASTIME OF PLEASURE (1509), as common wit, imagination, fantasy, estimation and memory. *10 serving thee* being your lover. *11 Who* which (his "foolish heart"). *11–12 leaves unsway'd . . . wretch to be* leaves the mere outward semblance of a man without a ruler in order to become your proud heart's slave and miserable vassal. The poet's heart (which should rule his body) has abandoned him to serve the heart of his mistress. *13 plague* affliction. *thus far . . . gain* I consider profitable to the following extent. *14 awards me pain* inflicts punishment upon me (in the act of sinning, and thus spares me a full measure of punishment thereafter).

SONNET 142. *1 dear* characteristic, especially valued. *2 Hate of . . . loving* hatred of my love (for you) because it is adulterous. *4 it* my state. *merits not reproving* does not desire to be reproved. *6 their scarlet ornaments* The lady's lips are equated with the red waxen seals upon such bonds as marriage contracts. *7 as mine* as my lips have done. *8 Robb'd . . . rents* cheated other wives of the marriage rights due to them. She has had affairs with other married men. *9 Be it* let it be. *13 what* i.e. pity. *hide* withhold. *14 self-example* the example you set.

141

In faith, I do not love thee with mine eyes,
For they in thee a thousand errors note;
But 'tis my heart that loves what they despise,
Who in despite of view is pleas'd to dote.
Nor are mine ears with thy tongue's tune delighted;   5
Nor tender feeling to base touches prone,
Nor taste, nor smell, desire to be invited
To any sensual feast with thee alone;
But my five wits nor my five senses can
Dissuade one foolish heart from serving thee,   10
Who leaves unsway'd the likeness of a man,
Thy proud heart's slave and vassal wretch to be.
    Only my plague thus far I count my gain,
    That she that makes me sin awards me pain.

142

Love is my sin, and thy dear virtue hate,
Hate of my sin, grounded on sinful loving.
O, but with mine compare thou thine own state,
And thou shalt find it merits not reproving!
Or if it do, not from those lips of thine,   5
That have profan'd their scarlet ornaments
And seal'd false bonds of love as oft as mine,
Robb'd others' beds' revenues of their rents.
Be it lawful I love thee as thou lov'st those
Whom thine eyes woo as mine importune thee.   10
Root pity in thy heart, that, when it grows,
Thy pity may deserve to pitied be.
    If thou dost seek to have what thou dost hide,
    By self-example mayst thou be denied!

143

SONNET 143. *1 careful* provident. *3 dispatch* haste. *5 holds her in chase* runs after her. *8 Not prizing* disregarding. *11 thy hope* that which you hope to catch. *13 thy Will* the man you are pursuing, presumably the poet's friend (with a quibble on the sense of "carnal desire").

SONNET 144. *1 of comfort and despair* one which offers comfort and the other which offers despair. Comfort (the hope for divine mercy) and despair are in theological terms the forces which vie for man's soul and lead to salvation or damnation. *2 suggest me still* continually urge me. *4 colour'd ill* (a) of dark complexion (b) of evil nature. *6 side* THE PASSIONATE PILGRIM, MALONE; Q: "sight." *8 foul pride* display of ugliness. *10 directly* clearly, unambiguously. *11 But being . . . each friend* but when they are both absent from me, each being friend to the other. *12 one . . . hell* i.e. they are engaged in sexual intercourse. *14 Till my . . . one out* until my evil angel has infected my good one with venereal disease.

143

Lo, as a careful housewife runs to catch
One of her feathered creatures broke away,
Sets down her babe, and makes all swift dispatch
In pursuit of the thing she would have stay;
Whilst her neglected child holds her in chase,   5
Cries to catch her whose busy care is bent
To follow that which flies before her face,
Not prizing her poor infant's discontent —
So runn'st thou after that which flies from thee,
Whilst I thy babe chase thee afar behind;   10
But if thou catch thy hope, turn back to me
And play the mother's part, kiss me, be kind.
    So will I pray that thou mayst have thy Will,
    If thou turn back and my loud crying still.

144

Two loves I have, of comfort and despair,
Which like two spirits do suggest me still.
The better angel is a man right fair,
The worser spirit a woman colour'd ill.
To win me soon to hell, my female evil   5
Tempteth my better angel from my side,
And would corrupt my saint to be a devil,
Wooing his purity with her foul pride.
And whether that my angel be turn'd fiend
Suspect I may, yet not directly tell;   10
But being both from me, both to each friend,
I guess one angel in another's hell.
    Yet this shall I ne'er know, but live in doubt,
    Till my bad angel fire my good one out.

SONNET 145. The poem is not a true sonnet, being written in octo-syllabic lines. Some critics have considered it to be a non-Shakespearean intrusion in the sequence. *1 Love's* Cupid's. *5 Straight* at once. *7 Was us'd . . . doom* was accustomed to pass gentle judgments. *8 greet* address me. *11 like a fiend* Night is conventionally referred to as the child of hell. *13 I hate . . . she threw* she removed the words "I hate" far from hatred, thus altering their meaning.

SONNET 146. *1 earth* body. The analogy of the human body to the physical earth is a Renaissance commonplace. *2 Fool'd by* MALONE; Q: "My sinfull earth," which is obviously repeated from the previous line. Malone's conjecture makes sense, as do various others which have been made to supply the two missing syllables. K indicates the hiatus without venturing a guess. *rebel . . . array* rebellious flesh that encloses you. *4 Painting . . . walls* adorning the body. *8 charge* object of your ex-penditure, the body. *9 upon . . . loss* by giving less to your servant, the body. *10 And let . . . thy store* and let the body suffer so as to increase your resources. That bodily privation increased the health of the soul was an ancient religious commonplace. *11 Buy terms . . . of dross* earn im-mortality in heaven by giving up sordid hours on earth. *12 without* on the outside. *13 So shalt . . . on men* in this way you shall conquer death, which destroys men.

146

Those lips that Love's own hand did make
Breath'd forth the sound that said "I hate"
To me that languish'd for her sake;
But when she saw my woeful state,
Straight in her heart did mercy come,　　　　5
Chiding that tongue that ever sweet
Was us'd in giving gentle doom,
And taught it thus anew to greet:
"I hate" she alter'd with an end
That follow'd it as gentle day　　　　10
Doth follow night, who, like a fiend,
From heaven to hell is flown away.
　　"I hate" from hate away she threw,
　　　And sav'd my life, saying "not you."

Poor soul, the centre of my sinful earth,
Fool'd by these rebel pow'rs that thee array,
Why dost thou pine within and suffer dearth,
Painting thy outward walls so costly gay?
Why so large cost, having so short a lease,　　　　5
Dost thou upon thy fading mansion spend?
Shall worms, inheritors of this excess,
Eat up thy charge? Is this thy body's end?
Then, soul, live thou upon thy servant's loss,
And let that pine to aggravate thy store;　　　　10
Buy terms divine in selling hours of dross;
Within be fed, without be rich no more.
　　So shalt thou feed on Death, that feeds on men,
　　　And Death once dead, there's no more dying then.

SONNET 147. *1 still* always. *2 nurseth* nourishes, keeps alive. *3 ill* illness. *4 Th' uncertain . . . to please* to cater to the fickle, unhealthy appetite (of the patient). *6 prescriptions* orders, instructions. *kept* followed. *7 I desperate* I who now am desperate. *7–8 approve . . . did except* now realize by experience that desire, which refused the help of reason's medicine, is fatal. *9 Past cure . . . past care* I can no longer be cured, now that reason has left me. *10 evermore* constant, eternal. *12 At randon . . . express'd* at variance from the truth and senselessly expressed. "Randon" is an old spelling of "random."

SONNET 148. *2 Which have . . . true sight* which see nothing as true sight would see it. *4 censures* judges, interprets. *aright* rightly. *5 false* distorting. *7 denote* indicate. *8 eye* There is a probable pun on "aye." *10 vex'd* afflicted. *watching* lying awake at night. *11 mistake my view* misjudge what I see. *13 Love* (a) Cupid, the god of love (b) the beloved lady. *14 foul faults* (a) physical ugliness (b) moral defects. *find* discover.

147

My love is as a fever, longing still
For that which longer nurseth the disease;
Feeding on that which doth preserve the ill,
Th' uncertain sickly appetite to please.
My Reason, the physician to my Love,   5
Angry that his prescriptions are not kept,
Hath left me, and I desperate now approve
Desire is death, which physic did except.
Past cure I am, now reason is past care,
And frantic-mad with evermore unrest;   10
My thoughts and my discourse as madmen's are,
At randon from the truth vainly express'd;
   For I have sworn thee fair, and thought thee bright,
   Who art as black as hell, as dark as night.

148

O me, what eyes hath Love put in my head,
Which have no correspondence with true sight!
Or, if they have, where is my judgment fled,
That censures falsely what they see aright?
If that be fair whereon my false eyes dote,   5
What means the world to say it is not so?
If it be not, then love doth well denote
Love's eye is not so true as all men's no.
How can it? O, how can Love's eye be true,
That is so vex'd with watching and with tears?   10
No marvel then though I mistake my view:
The sun itself sees not till heaven clears.
   O cunning Love! with tears thou keep'st me blind,
   Lest eyes well-seeing thy foul faults should find.

SONNET 149. *2 against . . . partake* take sides with you against my-self. *3-4 when I . . . thy sake* when I forget myself, complete tyrant, for your sake. Most editors agree that "tyrant" refers to the lady rather than to the poet, although the matter has been disputed. *7 low'r'st on* frown upon. *spend* mete out. *8 present moan* immediate suffering. *9 re-spect* discern. *10 so proud . . . despise* too proud to serve you. *11 de-fect* lack of good qualities. *12 motion* prompting, impulse. *14 Those that . . . am blind* Since the lady loves only those who can see her defects, her hatred of the poet constitutes a recognition of his blind passion.

SONNET 150. *2 With insufficiency* by virtue of your very shortcomings. *sway* rule. *3 give . . . sight* deny the truth of what I actually see. *4 that brightness . . . day* that it is not brightness that makes the day beautiful (and thus that it is darkness which does). *5 this becoming . . . ill* this power to make evil things seem good. *6 very . . . deeds* most worthless of your actions. *7 strength . . . skill* powerful assurance of excellence. *10 cause of* reason for. *13-14 If thy . . . of thee* if my passion is so strong that your defects can arouse love in me, I am all the more worthy of being loved by you.

Canst thou, O cruel! say I love thee not
When I against myself with thee partake?
Do I not think on thee when I forgot
Am of myself, all tyrant, for thy sake?
Who hateth thee that I do call my friend?   5
On whom frown'st thou that I do fawn upon?
Nay, if thou low'r'st on me, do I not spend
Revenge upon myself with present moan?
What merit do I in myself respect
That is so proud thy service to despise,   10
When all my best doth worship thy defect,
Commanded by the motion of thine eyes?
   But, love, hate on, for now I know thy mind:
   Those that can see thou lov'st, and I am blind.

O, from what pow'r hast thou this pow'rful might
With insufficiency my heart to sway?
To make me give the lie to my true sight
And swear that brightness doth not grace the day?
Whence hast thou this becoming of things ill,   5
That in the very refuse of thy deeds
There is such strength and warrantise of skill
That in my mind thy worst all best exceeds?
Who taught thee how to make me love thee more,
The more I hear and see just cause of hate?   10
O, though I love what others do abhor,
With others thou shouldst not abhor my state!
   If thy unworthiness rais'd love in me,
   More worthy I to be belov'd of thee.

SONNET 151. Some commentators have been shocked by the crude ob-
scenity of the double meanings in this sonnet. Shakespeare's contemporaries did not shy away from acceptance of normal bodily functions.
1 Love Cupid, a child. *conscience* awareness and understanding. In the
following line the word is used to suggest "guilty knowledge." *3 cheater*
betrayer (of all three men with whom she presumably has been involved).
urge . . . amiss charge me with my sin. *8 stays* waits for. *10 Proud of*
swelling with. *13 want of conscience* lack of awareness.

SONNET 152. *1 am forsworn* have broken an oath (the marriage vow).
2 art . . . swearing have broken two oaths since you have sworn love to
me. *3–4 In act . . . love bearing* i.e. you have broken one oath in your
violation of your marriage vow and another oath in your present rejection
of me after having sworn to love me. *bearing* professing. *7 misuse thee*
(a) misrepresent you, by calling you beautiful (b) use you wrongly, debauch
you. *8 And all . . . is lost* and in my dealings with you I have lost all
my integrity. *11 to enlighten . . . blindness* to make you seem bright,
pretended to see what I did not see. *12 swear against* deny. *13 eye* Q;
SEWELL, K: "I." The Q spelling leaves the intended pun sufficiently clear.

◇◇◇◇◇◇◇◇◇◇ 151

Love is too young to know what conscience is;
Yet who knows not conscience is born of love?
Then, gentle cheater, urge not my amiss,
Lest guilty of my faults thy sweet self prove.
For, thou betraying me, I do betray 5
My nobler part to my gross body's treason;
My soul doth tell my body that he may
Triumph in love; flesh stays no farther reason,
But, rising at thy name, doth point out thee
As his triumphant prize. Proud of this pride, 10
He is contented thy poor drudge to be,
To stand in thy affairs, fall by thy side.
 No want of conscience hold it that I call
 Her "love" for whose dear love I rise and fall.

◇◇◇◇◇◇◇◇◇◇ 152

In loving thee thou know'st I am forsworn,
But thou art twice forsworn, to me love swearing;
In act thy bed-vow broke, and new faith torn
In vowing new hate after new love bearing.
But why of two oaths' breach do I accuse thee 5
When I break twenty? I am perjur'd most;
For all my vows are oaths but to misuse thee,
And all my honest faith in thee is lost;
For I have sworn deep oaths of thy deep kindness,
Oaths of thy love, thy truth, thy constancy; 10
And, to enlighten thee, gave eyes to blindness,
Or made them swear against the thing they see;
 For I have sworn thee fair — more perjur'd eye,
 To swear against the truth so foul a lie!

SONNET 153. This and the following sonnet are unrelated to anything else in the sequence. They are variant free translations of a fifth-century Greek epigram by Marianus Scholasticus, first printed in Florence in the Planudean Anthology of 1494. It is unlikely that Shakespeare knew the Greek, however. The conceit was a familiar one that had appeared in many poems before his time. He may have found the epigram translated in Giles Fletcher's LICIA (1593). *1 brand* torch, with which Cupid enflames lovers. *2 maid of Dian's* nymph in the service of Diana, goddess of chastity. *advantage* opportunity. *4 of that ground* in that vicinity. *6 dateless* eternal. *still* forever. *7 seething* boiling. *yet* still. *prove* find to be. *10 for trial* to test its power. *11 withal* because of this. *12 hied* hastened. *distemper'd* sick. *14 eyes* MALONE; Q: "eye."

SONNET 154. *3 keep* observe. *5 votary* nymph who had sworn a vow of chastity. *7 general* leader, i.e. Cupid. *9 by* close by. *10 perpetual* eternal. *12 thrall* slave. *13 and this . . . prove* and I have learned and can demonstrate the following fact as a result of that experience.

154

✧✧✧✧✧✧✧✧✧✧ 153

Cupid laid by his brand and fell asleep.
A maid of Dian's this advantage found
And his love-kindling fire did quickly steep
In a cold valley-fountain of that ground;
Which borrow'd from this holy fire of Love   5
A dateless lively heat, still to endure,
And grew a seething bath, which yet men prove
Against strange maladies a sovereign cure.
But at my mistress' eye Love's brand new fired,
The boy for trial needs would touch my breast.   10
I, sick withal, the help of bath desired
And thither hied, a sad distemper'd guest,
    But found no cure. The bath for my help lies
    Where Cupid got new fire — my mistress' eyes.

✧✧✧✧✧✧✧✧✧✧ 154

The little Love-god, lying once asleep,
Laid by his side his heart-inflaming brand,
Whilst many nymphs that vow'd chaste life to keep
Came tripping by; but in her maiden hand
The fairest votary took up that fire   5
Which many legions of true hearts had warm'd;
And so the general of hot desire
Was sleeping by a virgin hand disarm'd.
This brand she quenched in a cool well by,
Which from Love's fire took heat perpetual,   10
Growing a bath and healthful remedy
For men diseas'd; but I, my mistress' thrall,
    Came there for cure, and this by that I prove —
    Love's fire heats water, water cools not love.

INDEX OF FIRST LINES

Index of First Lines

Accuse me thus: that I have scanted all	117
Against my love shall be as I am now,	63
Against that time (if ever that time come)	49
Ah, wherefore with infection should he live	67
Alack, what poverty my Muse brings forth,	103
Alas, 'tis true I have gone here and there	110
As a decrepit father takes delight	37
As an unperfect actor on the stage	23
As fast as thou shalt wane, so fast thou grow'st	11
A woman's face, with Nature's own hand painted,	20
Being your slave, what should I do but tend	57
Beshrew that heart that makes my heart to groan	133
Betwixt mine eye and heart a league is took,	47
Be wise as thou art cruel; do not press	140
But be contented. When that fell arrest	74
But do thy worst to steal thyself away,	92
But wherefore do not you a mightier way	16
Canst thou, O cruel! say I love thee not	149
Cupid laid by his brand and fell asleep.	153
Devouring Time, blunt thou the lion's paws	19
Farewell! thou art too dear for my possessing,	87
For shame, deny that thou bear'st love to any,	10
From fairest creatures we desire increase,	1
From you have I been absent in the spring,	98
Full many a glorious morning have I seen	33
How can I then return in happy plight	28

How can my Muse want subject to invent   38
How careful was I, when I took my way,   48
How heavy do I journey on the way   50
How like a winter hath my absence been   97
How oft, when thou, my music, music play'st   128
How sweet and lovely dost thou make the shame   95

If my dear love were but the child of state,   124
If the dull substance of my flesh were thought,   44
If there be nothing new, but that which is   59
If thou survive my well-contented day   32
If thy soul check thee that I come so near,   136
I grant thou wert not married to my Muse   82
I never saw that you did painting need,   83
In faith, I do not love thee with mine eyes,   141
In loving thee thou know'st I am forsworn,   152
In the old age black was not counted fair,   127
Is it for fear to wet a widow's eye   9
Is it thy will thy image should keep open   61

Let me confess that we two must be twain,   36
Let me not to the marriage of true minds   116
Let not my love be call'd idolatry   105
Let those who are in favor with their stars   25
Like as the waves make towards the pebbled shore,   60
Like as, to make our appetites more keen,   118
Lo, as a careful housewife runs to catch   143
Lo, in the Orient when the gracious light   7
Look in thy glass and tell the face thou viewest   3
Lord of my love, to whom in vassalage   26
Love is my sin, and thy dear virtue hate,   142
Love is too young to know what conscience is;   151

Mine eye and heart are at a mortal war   46
Mine eye hath played the painter and hath stell'd   24
Music to hear, why hear'st thou music sadly?   8
My glass shall not persuade me I am old   22
My love is as a fever, longing still   147

My love is strength'ned, though more weak in seeming; 102
My mistress' eyes are nothing like the sun; 130
My tongue-tied Muse in manners holds her still 85

No longer mourn for me when I am dead 71
No more be griev'd at that which thou hast done: 35
Not from the stars do I my judgment pluck, 14
No, Time, thou shalt not boast that I do change! 123
Not marble nor the gilded monuments 55
Not mine own fears, nor the prophetic soul 107

O, call not me to justify the wrong 139
O, for my sake do you with Fortune chide, 111
O, from what pow'r hast thou this pow'rful might 150
O, how I faint when I of you do write, 80
O, how much more doth beauty beauteous seem 54
O, how thy worth with manners may I sing 39
O, lest the world should task you to recite 72
O me, what eyes hath Love put in my head, 148
O, never say that I was false of heart, 109
Or I shall live your epitaph to make, 81
Or whether doth my mind, being crown'd with you, 114
O, that you were yourself! but, love, you are 13
O thou, my lovely boy, who in thy power 126
O truant Muse, what shall be thy amends 101

Poor soul, the centre of my sinful earth, 146

Say that thou didst forsake me for some fault, 89
Shall I compare thee to a summer's day? 18
Since brass, nor stone, nor earth, nor boundless sea, 65
Since I left you, mine eye is in my mind; 113
Sin of self-love possesseth all mine eye 62
So am I as the rich whose blessed key 52
So are you to my thoughts as food to life, 75
So is it not with me as with that Muse 21
Some glory in their birth, some in their skill, 91
Some say thy fault is youth, some wantonness; 96

So, now I have confess'd that he is thine   134
So oft have I invok'd thee for my Muse   78
So shall I live, supposing thou art true,   93
Sweet love, renew thy force; be it not said   56

Take all my loves, my love, yea, take them all!   40
That god forbid that made me first your slave   58
That thou are blam'd shall not be thy defect,   70
That thou hast her, it is not all my grief,   42
That time of year thou mayst in me behold   73
That you were once unkind befriends me now,   120
The forward violet thus did I chide: 99
The little Love-god, lying once asleep,   154
Then hate me when thou wilt! if ever, now!   90
Then let not winter's ragged hand deface   6
The other two, slight air and purging fire,   45
Th' expense of spirit in a waste of shame   129
They that have pow'r to hurt and will do none,   94
Thine eyes I love, and they, as pitying me,   132
Those hours that with gentle work did frame   5
Those lines that I before have writ do lie,   115
Those lips that Love's own hand did make   145
Those parts of thee that the world's eye doth view 69
Those pretty wrongs that liberty commits   41
Thou art as tyrannous, so as thou art,   131
Thou blind fool, Love, what dost thou to mine eyes 137
Thus can my love excuse the slow offence   51
Thus is his cheek the map of days outworn,   68
Thy bosom is endeared with all hearts   31
Thy gift, thy tables, are within my brain   122
Thy glass will show thee how thy beauties wear,   77
Tir'd with all these, for restful death I cry: 66
'Tis better to be vile than vile esteemed   121
To me, fair friend, you never can be old,   104
Two loves I have, of comfort and despair,   144

Unthrifty loveliness, why dost thou spend   4

Was it the proud full sail of his great verse,   86

Weary with toil, I hast me to my bed,   27

Were't aught to me I bore the canopy,   125

What is your substance, whereof are you made,   53

What potions have I drunk of Siren tears,   119

What's in the brain that ink may character   108

When forty winters shall besiege thy brow   2

When I consider every thing that grows   15

When I do count the clock that tells the time   12

When I have seen by Time's fell hand defaced   64

When, in disgrace with Fortune and men's eyes,   29

When in the chronicle of wasted time   106

When most I wink, then do mine eyes best see,   43

When my love swears that she is made of truth   138

When thou shalt be dispos'd to set me light   88

When to the sessions of sweet silent thought   30

Where art thou, Muse, that thou forget'st so long   100

Whilst I alone did call upon thy aid,   79

Whoever hath her wish, thou hast thy Will,   135

Who is it that says most which can say more   84

Who will believe my verse in time to come   17

Why didst thou promise such a beauteous day   34

Why is my verse so barren of new pride?   76

Your love and pity doth th' impression fill   112